Stepfamilies

Suzie Hayman is a counsellor, author and agony aunt and is the UK's leading expert on stepfamilies and their issues. She is Trustee and Spokesperson for Parentline Plus, the major UK parenting charity, and a trustee of the Who Cares Trust. She has been a stepmother for over thirty years.

Lion Television Scotland, a division of Lion Television, was set up in Glasgow to produce the award-winning *Castaway 2000* for BBC One. Since then the company has produced a wide range of programmes including *Time Commanders* and *Days That Shook The World.* Lion Television is a member of the All3Media Group.

Stepfamilies

Surviving and Thriving in a New Family

SUZIE HAYMAN

SIMON &
SCHUSTER

London • New York • Sydney • Toronto

First published in Great Britain by Simon & Schuster UK Ltd, 2005
A Viacom Company

10 9 8 7 6 5 4 3 2 1

Simon & Schuster UK Ltd
Africa House
64-78 Kingsway
London WC2B 6AH

www.simonsays.co.uk

Simon & Schuster Australia
Sydney

A CIP catalogue record for this book is available from the British Library

ISBN 0-7432-7601-9
EAN 9780743276016

Designed and typeset by Martin Lovelock

Printed and bound in Great Britain by The Bath Press, Bath

Contents

Thanks are due to:

All the families who took part in the BBC *Stepfamilies* series – your bravery and application are an inspiration to other families in this situation, showing us how it can work! It was a pleasure and a privilege to have spent time with you all.

The other families I have known over the years and whose stories I used – thank you, too.

All at Lion TV Scotland – the success of the help we offered our families really was a team effort.

San Lobel, my counselling supervisor, whose wisdom and good sense was invaluable.

And lastly but not least, the father of my stepson, my beloved stepson and his lovely wife. Couldn't have done any of it without you all!

Introduction

I estimate that in the UK as many as one in three people today are involved in some way in some sort of stepfamily. The traditional, mythical family of a couple who marry, have 2.4 children and stay together for the rest of their lives is becoming far from common. Families are increasingly diverse and it is estimated that, by 2010, the conventional idea of what makes a family will no longer hold true. The new norm will be groups of all shapes and sizes. Many of these will consist of singles, cohabiting couples, couples in the early stages of marriage without children and elderly couples whose children have flown the nest. The vast majority will be adults living in a married or unmarried relationship with children living with them or visiting, who may or may not be related to both those adults. Just how prevalent are such families, and the difficulties they often bring with them, was illustrated when I recently spoke about stepfamilies on a morning television programme. The presenters appealed for texts on the subject and the size of the response took the programme-makers – but not me – by surprise and totally overwhelmed their staff.

Official figures suggest that eleven per cent of families are stepfamilies. I think it's far, far more. Official figures may now count some couples who live together as well as married couples, but not all. Don't forget that for every couple caring for a child born to only one of the adults involved, there must be a parent outside this unit. A new partner for them, even if they only see the children briefly, is also a stepparent and part of a stepfamily but will not be counted in the figures, because the children are not resident with them. Grandparents are intimately and profoundly affected by having their children break up and reform their partnerships too, as are uncles and aunts, friends and colleagues. Ask among your circle of friends, look over your own family. If you're part of a stepfamily it's highly unlikely you're the only one. There are a lot of us about.

Families such as Tony and Nikki, who live with her son, 14-year-old Luke. Tony has two daughters aged 19 and 21. They live with their mother and stepfather and neither will speak to him. Or Sharon and Andy and her children, 11-year-old Josh and 3-year-old Rhiannon, and his children, 9-year-old Josh and 13-year-old Sian. Or Marian and Vic, who each have four children by their previous partners, and a child between them. Or Lynn and Tim, who live with her children Ryan, 13, and Rebecca, 10. Tim has a son, Matthew, whom he never sees but who is in the same class at school as Ryan. Or Denise and Ian who share a home with her children, 15-year-old Amy, 12-year-old Vikki and 11-year-old Sam. Oh – and not forgetting their shared child, 3-year-old Briana.

Sounds confusing? It is! It's been estimated that there are around seventy-two different forms of stepfamily. A divorced mother, whose ex is single, living with her children and a man previously unmarried with no children is one. Add a partner for the ex and you have another. Add an ex and children for this new partner and you have a third. Add an ex and kids for our original mother's new partner – well, you get the picture! With each new person in the family tree come fresh complications as new agendas, different emotions and often conflicting needs enter the arena.

What makes stepfamilies so very difficult is exactly this complexity. It's not like living in your traditional family – two parents with two kids and four grandparents. You can picture such a unit in the sort of family tree we're used to seeing – a straight up-and-down ladder that has clear outlines and a linear progression. This is the 'two up, two down' of families, like living in a terrace house; nice and simple, safe and easy to see and know who and where you are. Being in a stepfamily is more like inhabiting a sprawling estate with wings and attics and outbuildings, and skeletons in the cupboards and a mad aunt or two in the towers and all sorts of surprises lurking round every ramshackle corner. Stepfamilies are so hard because it's rarely easy to see the edge of your property, to know who belongs to whom, and what each of you may mean to each other. Living in such a rambling jumble can lead to your getting lost, to feeling frustrated and angry and left out. It's often tempting to blame one or two people in the mix for all the conflict and misery, or feel guilty that it's your own fault for it being so tricky.

Well, here's the good news. The truth is that it's the situation that makes it hard and it's the situation that is the main cause of the problems. And while you may not be able to actually change the basics of the situation, you can change how you feel about it, how you make sense of it and how you behave within it. You can't make other people change, but understanding their feelings and yours, their reactions and yours, may help all of you to reassess or behave differently.

Many of the difficulties stepfamilies face are common to all families. Toddlers will have tantrums, teenagers have bouts of moodiness, parents and children will quarrel whether they are mine, yours or ours. All families will have times of conflict and difficulties in agreeing and communicating. Most of the circumstances you encounter are not *problems* – which may be insurmountable – but *challenges*, that can be met. What research has shown is that it isn't divorce or living in a stepfamily that damages children or hurts adults. It's *badly managed* divorce and stepfamily living that does the harm. What leaves emotional scars is our not understanding what is happening and why, and not being able to see that there is a route through the mess and confusion.

This book will help you manage your family life better. As I tried to do in the BBC TV series *Stepfamilies*, this book will guide the reader through the difficulties, explain why certain things happen in stepfamilies and point to some workable solutions. I'll look at how you can surmount these arguments and build a family that has as much chance of being as happy as any first-time group, and that may have a considerable amount of 'added value' by virtue of the extra links and extra support that more people can bring to an extended family.

You come to a stepfamily with a lot of history. Obviously, no one enters even a first-time family with a totally clean sheet. The way you were brought up and the experiences you had as a child and a young person influence the way you find a partner and make a relationship. Your past can strongly affect the way your family develops. But while all families have a lot in common and just as much that makes each one unique and individual, all stepfamilies have one thing that both sets them apart from first-time families and unites them together. This is that they would not exist as a family at all if something awful hadn't happened. All stepfamilies are founded and based on a tragedy: someone has to have died or a relationship has to have come apart for them to be there. This simple fact sets off all the other problems – the unfinished business, the differing agendas, the issues over separate households and co-parenting and access and discipline – that are the stuff of stepfamily difficulties. And the subjects of this book.

During the TV series, viewers saw me use a variety of exercises and techniques to help families understand what is going on and also to bring a new family together. You'll find these and other techniques scattered throughout these pages, explained in more detail so that you can make use of them too.

Exercises and Techniques

You can pick and choose between:

- Family Answering Machine Message (does yours reflect everyone in the house?)

- Message Boards (a way of allowing all family members to claim territory and make themselves heard)

- Round table discussions (does everyone say their piece?)

- 'I' messages (a way of laying claim to your own feelings and making them heard from the heart)

- Genograms (an annotated family tree that reveals family patterns and often gives vital clues to what is happening)

- Negotiating, agreeing and writing up family contracts (say what you'll do and do what you say)

- Creating family chore charts (sharing the burden fairly)

- The Mantra (a way of putting your point in clear, non-confrontational terms using the formula 'when you ... I feel ... because ... what I would like is ...')

  ... and others

And who am I? Well, remember first of all that I make no claims to tell you what to do. My aim, whether it's face to face, on a telephone line, responding to a letter or email or in writing an article or book, is to try to understand what may be happening and why, and to help you do so too. On these pages I am distilling my experience and my training to explore the common issues stepfamilies go through. It's up to you to make use of it, to pick and choose what might be applicable to you, helpful to you and usable by you. However, I do believe I am particularly well placed to write on this subject. I'm a Relate trained counsellor and sometime agony aunt, and a trustee and spokesperson for Parentline Plus, the major parenting organization in the UK. Stepfamily issues feature large in both the letters and the emails I receive and in face-to-face counselling, and I am regularly asked to comment on the subject on radio, on TV and in the press. I'm also a stepmother, having been a third parent (Mum, Dad and 'Significant Other', as my stepson puts it) for over thirty years. As I have helped many hundreds of individuals and families during my career, as I hope I helped the families featured in the *Stepfamilies* series, I trust this book will be a guide for anyone reading it who is in or close to a stepfamily situation. I can't wave a magic wand and make it better for you. You'll have to do the work yourself to get anything out of this. Sometimes, just knowing why it's happening the way it is and that you're not the only one is enough to make life easier. I hope in these pages to give you a lot more, to enable you to turn your stepfamily around from the trial many people feel theirs to be, to the pleasure it can be. Please – read on!

Chapter 1

The Issues

All families are similar in some ways. We're all living with a range of personalities, trying to do our best and help each member get along with all the others. However hard we try, though, at times it doesn't go to plan. Whether you belong to a first-time or a second-time around family (or third or fourth!), you will find moments when life gets on top of you and you feel angry, overwhelmed or at a loss. The people who often give you joy and bring you comfort can get right up your nose, drive you crazy – up the wall and round the bend – and you may wonder why on earth you bother with them. Sharon says she felt it was like living in a war zone, Tracie was driven to tell her lot the wedding between her and Chris would be off if things went on the way they were, and Vic barred his eldest son from visiting him and his partner Marian, her four children and their shared child.

What usually produces pressure is change, whether small or large. A large change can be something such as moving house, losing a family member, starting a new school or job. Small changes can be something as simple as altering your eating habits or a new hairstyle. Every one of us, and all families, pass through what are called transitional points at set times. These are the moments when we move on from one stage in our own life, or the life of our family, to another stage. Learning to walk and talk, attending nursery, starting school, moving school, beginning to date, moving in with someone, pregnancy … All these are transitional points and such variations always mean you and those around you have to adjust and get used to the new order. Life is about constant adjustments, but it's natural to find them a bit of a shock and sometimes hard to manage. You may be delighted to begin a new life with someone, to move into a new home, to begin a new job, even to go on holiday – but however much you enjoy such modifications they also produce strain. We also call them crunch or pinch points – times when you feel brought up short and squeezed.

Stepfamilies have many similarities to first-time families, but they also have one overriding difference – a difference that binds all stepfamilies together, and sets them apart from all first-time families. To be there at all, something terrible has to have happened. There has to have been an ending – the death of a partner or a relationship – for you to be in this new family, a family that has in effect risen from the ashes of the previous one. Such a beginning leaves any stepfamily struggling with an extra measure of stress, in that many of the changes you have undergone are less than happy. In addition to all the natural crunch points any family might pass through, stepfamilies have to deal with a wide range of issues that are particular to second-time-around families, and which will affect you, everyone in your immediate, and often in your wider, family and circle. A first-time family, for instance, would have to make adjustments when a baby is born. However much the new arrival is planned and welcomed, it means new routines, a new status and new responsibilities. When two adults move in together and one or both bring children from a previous relationship, this process of adjustment is sudden and very complicated. You may go from having no children to being responsible for the welfare of a baby, a toddler, a teenager – with no prior experience or clear idea of what to do and how to do it. Sharon and Andy, for instance, went from being single parents with two children each to having four kids in a small three-bedroom house. Both had mixed feelings about the other's involvement in disciplining each other's children but both equally felt resentful at being left to cope with their own children on their own. Ade moved in with Vicky and her son Daniel and went from being single to being a partner and a Dad in one move.

How you deal with these issues will profoundly affect your family's and your ability to make this family unit work. The common issues that affect all stepfamilies form the main themes of this book. As well *Rising from the Ashes*, your family will have to deal with the *Unfinished Business and Baggage* that comes about because of the ending of a previous relationship. Just because you now live with someone else it doesn't mean your communication with or indeed your commitment to your former partner – or the arguments you ended on – are over. And you may also have to try to match up the very *Different Agendas* that various members of your family may have, with adults seeing the situation one way and wanting one thing, and children another. New adults may be struggling with *The Package Deal* – having fallen in love with and taken on an adult and not quite recognizing that Kids Come Too. Billy, for instance, paid his new partner Adele extravagant attention, buying her gifts and constantly wanting to take her out and whisk her away on holidays and weekends. He acted as if her two sons simply didn't exist, and eventually confessed that he'd be far happier if they went on one of their weekend visits to their father and never came back.

They may also be dealing with *Coming Late to the Scene* – learning to get on with and understand older children with a considerable history they do not share. Terri had a 2-year-old daughter and felt comfortable in her ability to deal with a young child, but totally at sea with her partner Ad's teenage daughter and son. We tend to assume that families have fairly simple forms – adults with two parents each and maybe two children between them. Stepfamilies often have very complex and sprawling shapes, so *Family Structures* – who belongs to whom and where do people fit in – can be a real concern. Vic confesses to sometimes getting confused as to who is who in his family, with his ex having four of his children and one by a former boyfriend as well as two stepchildren by her new partner, all of whom sometimes drop by to see him and consider him part of their lives.

Grandparents and Other Relatives are a common topic in stepfamilies. They may side with their own son or daughter and take against the other parent, making contact with their own grandchildren fraught and difficult. Sometimes they even lose contact – a distinct loss to children who may desperately need them as one solid aspect in a shifting universe. Rebecca refused to see her father Steve for some time, and in doing so also lost touch with his parents, her grandparents. Another important matter is often how to manage children moving between *Two Households* with different styles and rules. Tom lets his children stay up late and watch horror films when they stay with him, something his ex Jo and her new husband hate. How to make sure children do not *Lose Touch* with parents they no longer see every day is a key question – many dads, such as Barry, feel children won't come to any harm if the weekly visit has to be postponed a couple of times a month.

Stepfamilies frequently wrestle with *Names and Identity* – what children should call a new partner acting as a parent, and whether children should retain the name they might have been given at birth even when their own mother takes a new one. This can lead to arguments which in turn may cause adults to worry about *Discipline and Acting Out* – children who find it difficult to put their feelings into words behaving badly as a way of demonstrating that they feel bad. Many of these issues will come to a head around *Family Events – Festivals and Anniversaries*. Christmas or Chanukah or Eid, holidays and birthdays can all be stressful times and events around which conflict can focus.

The children's *School* can also be a hot issue. Some children find their school is a refuge and a place that can support them through difficult stepfamily times while others may feel being at school only adds to their stress. Little Josh does well at his school and has plenty of friends, while Ryan has gone through stages when he was on report for arguing. Some children behave like a dream at home and are holy terrors in school, some do it the other way round. Some schools would offer far more help and support if they were involved and informed about what might be happening at home, while others are given full information and fail to recognize the significance to their pupils' behaviour or needs. Above all, the *Image* of what a stepfamily is or should be can give rise to much heart-searching and worry, with adults and children feeling they 'ought' to be managing better, that people in their family 'should' be feeling or doing things differently.

Every stepfamily experiencing problems tends to think it's human error or malice that is at the root of them. It's a very common, human trait for us to look for someone to blame when things go wrong or feel uncomfortable. We either think that we, as the adults in charge, are uniquely incompetent and it's all our fault this isn't working, or we convince ourselves that it's the kids, or other adults, concerned that are uniquely awful and conspiring to make the situation so hard. Tim, for instance, was sure that his stepson Ryan was the problem in his family, because he seemed to be the one at the bottom of most of the arguments. Since Ryan would often come home from visits with his

Negotiating

One vital skill to learn when considering a stepfamily is How to Negotiate.

Negotiation means coming to an agreement with everyone happy with what's been decided. It might seem to take a bit longer than simply putting your foot down, but in the long run it's quicker, works better and leaves everyone happy.

How do you negotiate?

Someone makes a demand – 'I am going to see my Dad tomorrow.'

Gather information – 'Did he ask you? What's the plan?'

Discuss – 'Well, no, he didn't. but I really want to.' 'I think he said he was away this week, darling. But let's ring him and see.'

Come to mutual understanding and agreement – 'If he can't see you tomorrow, what about Friday?'

What helps and what gets in the way of negotiation?

It holds you back if

- You think you know what your child should do, and are sure you're right.

- You make judgements about your child or what they want.

- You let your own feelings, of fear or anger or envy, get in the way.

It helps if

- You listen without interrupting.

- You give your child your full attention.

- You really want to understand what your child is feeling and needing, and let them know that.

- You keep checking out that you understand what is wanted and what is going on.

father Steve in a bad mood, Tim was also certain Steve must be 'calling' or criticizing him and Ryan's mother Lynn and that he was the author of many of their troubles. Sharon was sure that her new partner Andy's son Josh was the root of all the stress and tension. He would give her dirty looks, she said, and was constantly messing about with and upsetting Sharon's daughter Rhiannon.

In fact, the emotions and behaviours felt and shown in these families and many others are universal, and come about for very normal and natural reasons. Rather than being the result of deliberate goading or spite, they are understandable reactions to a difficult situation. My belief is that once we can understand what those issues are, we can manage them. That is what this book is all about.

But we shouldn't assume that all the problems you encounter in a stepfamily are about stepfamily issues. Don't forget that sometimes the problems may be more about one of those transitional points. They would have happened even in a first-time family. All toddlers go through the Terrible Twos, all teenagers have to rebel, and all loving, happy, committed couples have times when they argue and don't see eye to eye. Being in a stepfamily may give the problem an extra slant – a weight or dash of guilt or level of difficulty – but you may need to tease out and separate one from the other in order to properly address it.

Perfection is a snare and a delusion. Nobody is perfect, and striving to be the perfect parent or stepparent with the perfect family or child is where most people come to grief. We don't come up to scratch because we're only human, and then struggle further with feelings of anger, guilt, incompetence and failure. What we should all be aiming for is '**Good Enough Parenting**' – simply doing the job to the best of our ability and being happy and content in it. Most important of all, there is no one right way to be either a parent or a stepparent, although one important key is seeing a stepparent as an additional adult and not a replacement for a missing parent.

There are a variety of skills needed in a parenting role of any sort. You need to be able to:

- See things from the point of view of the children.

- See the point of negotiation, and to do it.

- Listen and let people express their feelings and opinions.

- Be optimistic, creative and open to new ways of doing things.

This book, I hope, will help you do all of them!

Things to Keep in Mind

- Don't look for blame, look for solutions.

- Be aware that all stepfamilies have certain issues – things that set them apart from first-time families, and that you hold in common with all stepfamilies.

- Learn to recognize the transition or change points in everyone's life – passing from courting to settled couple, children going from primary to secondary school, a family member dying. Be prepared for there to be difficulties at such times.

- Discuss the compromises you are all going to have to make over such major issues as discipline and family routines *before* you move in together – or start to do so *now*.

- Do health checks on the relationships between you and all the other family members – exs, grandparents etc – who are involved in your new stepfamily arrangements.

- Don't assume your difficulties are necessarily about your being a stepfamily. Your problems could be about something in your earlier life which wasn't dealt with at the time.

- Nobody is or can be perfect. Being 'good enough' is the realistic goal.

Chapter 2

Rising from the Ashes

A second marriage is, as Samuel Johnson said, 'the triumph of hope over experience'. And that's what most of us have when we find ourselves in a stepfamily – a feeling of triumph that we may be starting again, and lots of hope that whatever experiences may have led us to be in this situation will now contribute to a 'happy ever after'. Our optimism may carry us through and help us make it work. But the fact that this new relationship is, for at least one of us, a return rather than a first time may mean that unless we at least consider the significance of that fact, we could be heading for trouble.

Nobody goes into even a first-time family with a completely blank sheet. It's highly unlikely that either of you will have reached this point in your lives with no past loves, no past entanglements. There will have been boy- or girlfriends, people you dated semi-seriously or seriously. And you will have had sexual liaisons and perhaps lived with someone or several someones. But if this is a stepfamily, either or both of you have gone more than one step further. You will have linked up with another person – the other parent of your child or children.

And with that, even fleeting, connection you will have formed hopes and expectations and looked forward to a life with the other parent of those children. Those hopes have been dashed, that expectation has been sunk. Stepfamilies and first-time families have much in common, but one thing separates them, and unites all stepfamilies. This is that each and every stepfamily is built in the ruins of a previous family; the death of a person or a relationship. Loss always gives rise to feelings of despair, shock, grief, guilt, rage, anxiety and depression, and we'll deal with these in a later chapter. For now, you need to see that part of the reason for going into a new relationship is the urge to climb above the sadness of the past. To rise, in effect, from the ashes.

Going into a stepfamily gives you tremendous hopes for getting it right the second time around, both in your one-to-one relationship with your new partner and in the way you manage being a parent. Ali, for instance, had little contact with his own children after the break-up with his ex-wife. His son was 11 and his daughter 14 when he left ten years ago. His daughter is now married and his son at college and neither welcomed his approaches for many years. When Ali remarried Sonia, who had two children of her own, he was determined to do a better job of being a stepfather than he had as a father. Ali tried hard, and with Sonia's support and the help of a counsellor he made a good relationship with his stepchildren and their father. When he heard that his daughter was engaged, he decided to see if he could do better by his original family too, having seen how

How to Reconnect

If you want to get in touch, or start again when contact has gone sour, you could make the first contact by letter. Write, saying clearly what you'd like and how much you regret having lost touch. Don't assign blame and don't start an argument, but ask if you can put the past aside to do better in the future. If you think it might help, offer to meet again with the support and guidance of a counsellor or mediator. Above all, make clear you want this to be hopeful and helpful and will do your best to make it so.

positive efforts could pay off. He got in touch and tried hard to build bridges with them – an attempt that was at first rebuffed but then allowed. Now he not only has the satisfaction of having a loving family with his stepchildren but also has renewed contact with his son and daughter, and his new grandchild.

A new family can give you the incentive to do better by your children – those who live with you, those who don't and those who may not have any blood link but have become yours. Rising from the ashes gives you a chance to be redeemed, both as a parent and a partner. Lee had had three relationships that were serious – two in which he had children – before meeting Carly. Lee appeared a very confident, if not cocky, man, but underneath he lacked self-esteem and was sure the relationship breakdowns had been his fault and proved he was a failure. Carly showed him that laying blame was a waste of effort – what mattered was what you were going to do about it now. There were elements of Lee's behaviour that had contributed to the breakdown of his former relationships, and that put his present one at risk. One was his assumption that women did all the housework, in spite of the fact that both he and Carly worked full-time. Another his habit of walking away when an argument started rather than trying to sort out what was going wrong. Instead of laying blame, Carly asked him to take responsibility – responsibility for his actions and responsibility for making changes. Because he was certain he didn't want another relationship to fail and wanted this one to both last and make amends for the earlier mistakes, he did.

Starting a stepfamily is being given a **second chance at family life**, knowing what you know now. Although many churches, and charities such as Relate, do offer pre-marriage workshops and some schools now look at families and how they work, the fact is that there is no manual and no 'driving test' you are required to study or take before embarking on the most difficult yet most rewarding adventure of your life – making a relationship. And babies don't come with manuals either – you get handed yours, and you're on your own. So your first-time partnership and your first-time family may have been the place you made all your mistakes. And why should you have been any better at it? You weren't trained or skilled. But now, going into a second relationship, you have some know-how. You can build on past experiences. It's a bit like being able to do all those school exams all over again, but this time with hindsight and practice and an insight into what works and what doesn't.

Rising from the ashes can help you overcome fears of having been a failure as a parent and partner. If you can get it right this time, you can see that all sorts of influences may have hindered you from making a success before. Many of them are things you can work on now but none of them are things you should beat yourself up over for the past. And you may be able to approach this new family with a sense of realism – you know what you need to do or expect to make a family work. It doesn't 'just happen' – it takes work and effort, and you know that now.

No Blame

I often tell people 'This isn't a blame-laying exercise …' What it might be, however, is an opportunity to recognize your responsibility for the way things happen in your relationships and family. It isn't your fault if you have grown up thinking the way to parent is to punish first and listen a poor second. Or that the way to deal with disagreements is to shout, or to turn your back. It's not your fault and you aren't to blame – these and others are behaviour patterns we learn from our own upbringing and background. But they aren't helpful. Reading a book like this, discussing with our partners and family and sometimes taking counselling are ways to learn and listen and change. You have the opportunity to chose to be different and to do it better. Take it!

The downside to trying to make a new family on the foundation of an old one is that instead of learning from those old mistakes, you may simply repeat them. Maybe you and your previous partner walked away from your last family without really addressing what went wrong. Because you didn't take the opportunity to understand, you can't make the changes necessary to prevent you doing the same thing again. And when problems do arise, you may make the instant assumption of 'Oh, oh – here we go again; we're doomed!' Seeing a repeat of certain behaviour may derail you, as you expect the new family to go the way of the old and to founder whatever you do, when otherwise it might have succeeded.

We will be looking in more detail later at how the way you ended your previous relationship can affect your present one. For now, it's worth considering that how you have entered this new one may have put you in a vulnerable or a strong position. Trying again too early – getting back up on the bike before you lose your nerve – may mean you are on the rebound. The problem with having come from a relationship that you might not have expected to finish is that you sometimes find yourself making assumptions about new relationships. You're so used to having someone in your life, to being part of a couple, that when you start dating you may fall into the habit of treating your new partner in many ways like the old one – taking it for granted this will be a relationship that lasts and that gives you certain privileges with each other. You may find you have fast-forwarded to live-in coupledom quicker than you might have if this had been a relationship you had made earlier in your life. Sharon and Andy, for instance, met in a nightclub and in a very short time moved in together. Part of the rush was because her son Josh was about to move up from primary to secondary school. It seemed to make sense for them to put their families together and for her and her children to move to his part of the country to coincide with this, rather than have Josh start at a new school and then have to uproot. But the problems they experienced in trying to put two families together were not helped by the fact that they had a limited history together, only having gone out with each other for a short period before becoming not only a couple but a family.

Sometimes **jumping ahead into being a family** is because of your own internal feelings and needs. Sometimes you take that step because of other people's pressures or presumptions. Friends and family may put pressure on you to have another person in your life because they want you partnered and looked after. It makes life simpler for them if they don't have to feel they should be responsible for your well-being! Or they may hurry you into it by being hostile and against it, making you eager to prove them wrong. You may spring into being a serious couple simply because dating feels so awkward. That long slow getting-to-know-you phase of a relationship only feels right when you're a teenager with no ties. It feels awkward when you are a grown-up with kids of your own. And there is the simple fact of not having the time or the space to date as you might have done when there were no children around. You can't spend weekends together or decide to go out on the town when there are kids to consider. Your fear that they may be confused by a succession of boy- or girlfriends can have you jumping the gun as you might not have done if you were single and childfree.

This hurrying into it can provoke some problems. In rising from the ashes, you may find yourself trying to gloss over some aspects of the past. Noah and Mia met when her son Jason was just over a year old and her daughter Keri was 6. Their father had walked out and had no contact with them at all. From the beginning, Jason welcomed the new man in the house and, when he started to talk, called him Dad. Mia's daughter was more wary, but did get on well with Noah, calling him by his name. Problems started when Keri was 10

– a baby came along and she suddenly realized that she was the only one in the family who seemed alone and without a dad of her own. The fact that her now 5-year-old brother wasn't Noah's son had become a family secret – something no one talked about out loud, even some of their close friends didn't know and their family seemed to have forgotten, and that was kept hidden from the boy himself. The scene was set for an almighty blow-up when Keri finally got fed up with her brother making fun of her for not having a dad, and told him neither did he.

Being determined to do better and make good on the past by treating your stepchildren well can also backfire on you if it means your birth children feel that in doing so you short-change them. Rebecca, for instance, felt aggrieved that her father Steve tried to be fair and not neglect his new partner's children in favour of her and her brother Ryan. To her, this meant that she wasn't given her special due as his own daughter, especially since it seemed to her that he went with little explanation from living with them to living with the new family. She felt personally abandoned and rejected, and responding by rejecting and abandoning him, refusing to see him and saying she never wanted to see him again.

The mechanics of starting and running a relationship when one or both of you have kids can be complicated, to say the least. To encourage any relationship, you need to **find time for yourselves as a couple**. To make any family work, you need to devote time to each child individually and to the family as a whole. This is all very well when you begin a first-time relationship and there are only the two of you to consider; children come along after a time and you can grow up with them. It doesn't work when you or your partner are acquiring an instant, often quite grown-up, family. Noah and Mia struggled to make time for themselves, since babysitters were in short supply, Jason and Kerri never spent time with their father, and both their families lived

Making a Promise

Some families are deciding to make a commitment between new partner and child as much a part of the vows as those between the new couple during a wedding ceremony. It underlines the fact that when you link up with someone who has children, they are necessary part of the relationship. When Les married Sue these are the vows he and her son Kai exchanged:

Les to Kai

Kai, when I met your mummy just over three years ago, I knew she had a son. What I didn't know was how important that son would become to me.

I have watched you grow from a six-year-old boy to who you are today. Some of the best memories I have are the fun we have all had together. The best is when Mummy is not around so she cannot interrupt our PlayStation games!

My promise to you is this – I look forward to being a big part of your life as you continue to grow up. I will always be here for you – as your stepdad, but first of all as your friend. I will respect your opinions, and cherish our times together. Don't hesitate to come to me about anything – whether good or bad, and I will do everything I can to help you.

I love you, Kai, and I am so happy the three of us are becoming a new family.

Kai to Les

Les, I think you'll do great as my stepfather. Since you and Mummy got together, we have all been happier. I like when you play with me, and you make me laugh. I hope we get to do lots more picnics and camping together.

I promise to listen to you, and respect you. You are doing great so far. I thank God for helping us find each other so we can all become a new family.

I love you, Les. You mean the world to me.

far away so couldn't offer to give them time for themselves. Even when children don't live with you, you still have responsibilities to them, and a new relationship may be hampered by the need to spend every weekend with your children from a previous relationship rather than the two of you on your own. Carlos and Fi realized after a year together that they had never once had a weekend on their own. His children came to stay with him every weekend and one night a week too. This can mean that couples have difficulty laying the foundations for a strong, caring and sound relationship, something that comes from being able to spend time and effort on each other. If you've had to snatch hurried time for yourselves in between caring for his or her kids, when trouble does arise you may not be able to stand shoulder to shoulder together against it. Ade and Vicky had little time for courting. They met through a dating agency and moved in together very quickly. Not only did they have little time alone because of Vicky's son Daniel, within a few months their own twins, Benjamin and Thomas, were on the way. They lived together, they had children together but they had hardly any communication or time together. And the sad truth is that children who have no other way to make their feelings known can often seize on such a chink in your armour. They may exploit this lack of unity, this inability to work together as one, to drive you apart and turn you against each other.

You as an individual and you as a couple need to look after yourselves and your relationship. When you're trying to keep a new family together, it's very easy to feel overwhelmed and believe there simply isn't time to fritter away on yourselves. But if you don't keep yourself and your personal relationship healthy, your family suffer as well as you. Make time to go out at least once a week as a couple – you deserve it and need it. If money is short for babysitters, link up with other parents and form a babysitting ring. Or shamelessly exploit your family to help you out. In addition, take my words on CARE FOR THE CARER to heart – copy it out and stick it on your fridge!

When and how you **introduce children to a new partner** is a delicate balancing act. Keeping kids a secret from a new love means starting the relationship off on a lie. And keeping your love-life hidden from your children until a surprise breakfast tray gets dumped into the wrong lap one Sunday morning could be disastrous. But avoid the temptation to fix up jolly days at the zoo in the first few months – everyone needs time to get used to the idea. New families cope better when you have told your date about your kids, your kids about your date from the beginning. Both need to know the other exists but you don't need to plan weddings or a lifetime of living together immediately. Make a first meeting between your date and your children casual and quick and increase time together by minutes rather than hours over a period of weeks. When the time comes for you to think about going any further, let them know what you have decided. Some parents wonder whether they should be asking their children about such changes, which after all will affect them deeply. My personal view is that you should keep your children in the loop, ask their opinions and feelings (and be prepared for these to be negative) but not put the burden of making decisions on them. It's your choice to bring a new adult into your and their life, and your responsibility to make sure it's good for them as well as good for you. You can't be expected to be in mourning for a past love, a past family, all your life. Sooner or later, you and your family need to move on and make new relationships. But you do need to take on board the very different feelings they will have about this. And you certainly do need to maintain their links with their original family, even if you both desire and need to move on – on that, more later. Rising from the ashes doesn't mean shaking all the dust of the past off your shoes.

Care for the Carer

If you're someone who makes a habit of looking after other people you may forget to look after yourself, or to allow others to care for you. It's really important to recognize that you need and deserve care, too. And that you take the time and effort to give yourself as much help as you are offering other people. So take this advice to heart:

- Be gentle with yourself!

- Remind yourself that you are not a magician. You can't work miracles.

- Recognize that other people's problems are their property and their responsibility, not yours. You can't fix everything, nor should you try.

- Give support, encouragement and praise. Learn to accept it in return.

- Change your routines often and your tasks when you can.

- Learn to recognize the difference between complaining that offloads and makes you feel better, and complaining that just reinforces stress.

- Focus on one good thing that happened today.

- Schedule 'withdraw' periods at least twice a week when you can be calm and at peace and no one interrupts you.

- Say 'I choose' rather than 'I should' or 'I ought to' or 'I have to' or 'I must'.

- Say 'I won't' rather than 'I can't'.

- Say NO sometimes – you can't do everything. If you never say NO, what is your YES worth?

- Being aloof, distant or indifferent is far more hurtful and harmful than admitting you can't cope.

- Give yourself permission to have fun – often!

I like it when …

If you saw the TV series *Stepfamilies* you would have seen the families doing an exercise that was great fun but also had a point. It involved a large ball of ribbon but you can do the same with a ball of string or wool.

Gather round in a circle. Take a ball of string or wool, and agree or toss for who goes first.

The first person keeps hold of the end of the string and passes the ball to someone else in the circle, saying 'I like it (or I liked it) when we (or you) …' It could be something such as 'I like it when you take me for a walk with the dog,' or 'I liked it when we played games last weekend,' or 'I like it when you help me with my homework.'

The first person and this second person are now connected by a length of string. The second person keeps hold of their section, and in turn passes the ball to someone else in the circle, also saying 'I like it (or I liked it) when we (or you) …' The second person is now also connected to the third person, who in turn does the same thing. You can pass it to anyone you like, except the person who has just passed it to you. You can come back to the person who gave it to you last when the ball comes round to you again from someone else. Try to pass the ball on to everyone at least once, and try to think of as many nice things as possible to keep it going.

When you finally run out of things to say, have a look at what you have. It should be a spider's web of string that criss-crosses the room to tie you all together. You might have thought your stepfamily was divided and unrelated – and yet, here is a pattern of connections, holding you together. You may find that reassuring. You may need to look at who is connected to whom; those who have the fewest lines between them may need some support and help to strengthen their links and so build up the stepfamily.

Things to Keep in Mind

- A stepfamily is always the result of someone's loss. Expect to have to go back and do some mourning before you reach the 'happy ever after' part.

- A stepfamily can be a second chance for everyone involved. Take a long, hard look at any past mistakes and make efforts not to repeat them.

- Become a stepfamily for the right reasons – because you love the other adult and accept Children Come Too. If you or your new partner are 'on the rebound' or you link up in spite of the children, you may be in for a bumpy ride.

- Introduce your children gradually to any potential new partner. But don't give them the burden of making a choice – that decision is yours.

- Make time for yourselves as a couple. You have a new relationship to build and firmly establish as well as a new stepfamily.

- Make a point of doing things that bring you together as a family, too. Eat your evening meal around a table, play board games on one night a week, go out together for a walk or to kick a football around, do the weekly shop all together.

- Call on any help from friends, family and professionals you can get to try to make your stepfamily come together from the very beginning. You are taking on a difficult task and will need and deserve such assistance.

Chapter 3

Unfinished Business and Baggage

When the hero – or, increasingly, the heroine – gets socked on the jaw in the movies, they simply shake their head, leap up and continue as if nothing had happened. In real life, you'd have concussion or a broken jaw and probably need to sit down, burst into tears, throw up or all three. When a relationship finishes we seem to think we can shake our heads, leap up and continue as if nothing has happened. In reality, it's not like that at all.

Whatever your role in the ending of a relationship, it leaves a mark. It may happen through the choice of neither of you – your partner might have died. Increasingly, however, partnerships are ended when one or other or both of you together decide to call it a day. Anne left her husband Mark because, after four years of steadily increasing misery, she finally realized she had fallen out of love with him. There was no one else in the equation – she simply didn't love him any more and couldn't bear to live with him under those circumstances even though he was content to carry on as they were. Matt, on the other hand, had an affair with his wife Donna's best friend. Donna, he thought, hadn't paid him any attention since their son was born and he felt neglected and rejected. As far as Donna was concerned, the split came as a complete shock – Matt had taken her on a 'romantic' break to Paris for her birthday ten days before announcing he was leaving. Smita and Ajay agreed it was time to call a halt when both accepted that their relationship had run aground. Neither could bear to be in the same house, let alone room, with each other, and their constant rows were scaring their children.

Whether chosen or unwanted, foreseen or unexpected, the **ending of a family** leaves unfinished business for everyone. Adults may be left with grief, over a relationship they thought was working or that still had some life and hope in it coming to an end. They may battle with confusion, that their partner saw it in a different light. Or anger, at being betrayed. Or guilt, if it was they who decided to leave. There may be resentment at deceit and lies or at being neglected. Frequently, both parties are left feeling their side of the story hasn't been heard or understood – that the argument was stopped or put aside before they had their full say. For children, the unfinished business is even more acute. Whatever the arguments, and indeed however bad a job parents may doing, children want the family to remain unchanged, together and at home for them, forever. Breaking up usually leaves them with a sense of the floor shifting, the sky falling, the world at odds. Indeed, even grown-up children can feel bereft when their parents part – we never get over the wish to have Mum and Dad together. If there has been violence or bitter disputes, children may be relieved when it appears to end and parents go separate ways. But given the choice, children will say they wished the arguments could have been resolved and the family could have stayed intact. They may also often not understand why their parents are separating, particularly if parents feel it isn't appropriate to explain the private details of their own decisions. While it isn't right to tell a child, 'Daddy has had an affair,' or 'Mummy prefers someone else to Daddy,' saying nothing may leave them to fill the absence with their own imaginings – such as 'I wasn't good enough so Daddy decided he didn't want to be with me any more.'

This **hangover from the past** is probably the basic and most important issue for stepfamilies and the one at the root of most stepfamily difficulties. Much as you may want to believe or persuade yourself that you can forge on and forget it, you simply can't turn your back, walk away and ignore what got you there in the first place. Stuff from your previous union and stuff from the ending of it carries over into the next relationship. Very few people can calmly sit down, have it out and be done with the resentments and quarrels that might have grown during their relationship and that will certainly have accumulated around its ending. Most of us carry on with some 'leftovers'. You may have moved yourselves to another location and no longer live under the same roof. What you haven't been able to do is cut the real ties that bind you.

The unfinished business may show itself in continuing arguments and conflict between you and your ex. You might think once a relationship is over, that's that. In reality, separated couples often go on being tied together as strongly when they live apart as they were when they lived together. There may seem to be all sorts of good reasons why you go on being in touch, and go on arguing as you did before you split up. There may still be money owed by both of you, or by one to the other, or property you still haggle over. You may have mutual friends or acquaintances, especially if you live in the same area. The most common and obvious reason, of course, is that you have to continue to see each other because you have children between you. While you are no longer *partners*, you continue to both be *parents*. Your kids need to see the missing parent, so you need to see them when you hand over children for a visit, or must contact them to discuss when access will happen, where and how. You also need to be in touch to discuss matters about your children –

medical, financial, educational, emotional – that need both parents' input. And this can often become a focus for arguments, with each parent blaming the other or new partners for any unhappiness or conflict that comes to light in or with the children.

The unfinished business can also affect the way you deal with **new relationships**. You may feel wary or suspicious, or jump to conclusions from behaviour you see in them that reminds you of things your ex did, or does. When Donna started seeing Paul she found herself getting upset and argumentative every time he was late because he'd stopped after work to have a drink with his friends. Even though he was only half an hour late, and phoned her from the bar, she flew off the handle and then sulked. It took some time for her to realize it was her ex, Matt, she was angry at, and Matt she had had reason to distrust, not Paul.

Unfinished business can come between you and your children. Lynn and her son Ryan had steadily escalating arguments over the four years after she left Ryan's father, Steve , for her new partner, Tim. Ryan was angry about the way he felt his mother and stepfather had conducted their affair, seeing each other while Lynn and Steve were still together instead of waiting until they had separated. As far as Ryan was concerned, Lynn had betrayed him as much as she had betrayed Steve and he couldn't let go of this anger. Parents such as Abiba also may find that a child who strongly resembles or identifies with a missing partner can set their teeth on edge. Her daughter Nasha seemed the image of her missing father in her looks and her personality – strong-willed, argumentative – and constantly talked about him and referred to him. Every time the little girl answered back, Abiba found herself taking out her resentment over the break-up on the child.

For the adults, who are separating from a partner, the best solution may seem to be to draw a line under the relationship and move on. For the children, the only acceptable solution is to remain in close touch with both parents. Managing these two disparate needs is the key to having a happy stepfamily, but it's often very difficult. Andy, for instance, became furious when he thought his partner, Sharon, was being friendly with or spending any time with her ex, Michael. He accepted her children's need to see their father but felt she should drop them off and have no face-to-face contact herself. He couldn't understand why she needed to talk with him, and his insistence troubled her and confused the children.

It's a common situation for adults to have feelings of anger and resentment for an ex-partner. Equally common is the resentment or jealousy felt by a new partner for the other parent of their partner's children. Sometimes this is because they feel defensive about the person they love, and are angry at the pain and hurt they feel the ex has caused them or their new partner's children. Donna's new partner, Paul, hated her son seeing his father, Matt, and said it was because he had been a terrible father. Having had an affair, Matt might not be seen as the best partner, but in fact he tried hard after the separation to be a good parent to his son.

In many cases, though, it's anxiety at the role an ex can play in the new relationship that makes for conflict. Andy, like many new partners, was jealous and nervous about any contact with Sharon's ex. He was afraid that if he couldn't get it right with Sharon, she might give in to her son Josh's longing and reunite with Josh's father, Michael. New partners often feel that keeping the offending exes away will keep out the risk they seem to pose to the new family. The danger can be explained as physical or emotional harm to the ex-partner or children from violence, threats or arguments. Or it can be seen as a risk of temptation, as old partners may seek to lure an ex back by working on the children. In new families, any sign of the old or a non-residential parent is often banned. Photos of the old family, pictures of missing parents, are either thrown away, doctored or hidden in drawers or attics.

The problem is that the boundaries have already been breached, the outside world has already entered into the new home, in the shape of the children themselves. They are the living, walking proof that someone else was there first and still exists, however distantly. In seeking to bar entrance, the new partner or the parent passes on one very confusing and worrying message to the children concerned: seeing their missing parent as dangerous, undesirable, unwanted also tells them they are dangerous, undesirable, unwanted too. After all, their missing parent forms a part of them. This makes children feel uncomfortable and unhappy. It also manages to bring the dangerous outside into the new family rather than keeping it out. Opposition to a missing parent may make the parent and their lifestyle even more desirable to the children concerned – talking about or hankering after them becomes a handy way of showing rebellion. Or it makes the child refused access to a missing parent feel upset, confused and guilty.

Instead of actually banning contact, some separated parents and stepparents try other means of **breaking the link**. Knowingly or unknowingly, they may seek to make the parent living away from their child seem like a bad lot, by talking about them in front of the children and heaping all the blame for the situation on them. Tim, like many stepparents or parents with whom their children live, was in the habit of criticizing the non-resident parent. He did so feeling he had a right and that his criticism was justified, particularly since it was mainly about Steve's shortcomings in being a father to his children. There had been a period during which Steve had little contact with his kids, especially his daughter. And he seldom phoned midweek, in between seeing them. What Tim, like many people, didn't recognize was the effect his criticism had on his stepchildren. As far as a child is concerned, 'a parent is a parent for all that'. It doesn't matter what they might have done – 'That's still my dad or my mum you're dissing.' And in doing so, you call into question several things about the child themselves.

- You question their loyalty and their instincts because you ask them to betray the love they feel for their parent.

- You ask them to go against their natural inclination to unconditionally love their parents.

- You question the security they get from feeling a parent is always there for them.

- You also pass judgement on the child, in passing judgement on the adult.

Children know that it took their two parents to make them, that they are in effect a combination of the two. Disapprove of a parent and you disapprove of that part of them; whatever you say against the parent they will take as being aimed at and belonging to them also. They take it personally – and are right in doing so. Children can strongly identify with their parents. Ryan, for instance, felt after the break-up of his family that he had been the one lied to, cheated and betrayed as well as, or even rather than, his father. He was angry with his mother, and his outbursts against her were so particularly bitter because he had taken upon himself the feelings that you might have expected his father to have over his wife's infidelity. Many young people in Ryan's position will feel the same – that a hurt to a parent is a hurt to them, too. Of course, some children take the opposite stand. A parent's or stepparent's criticism of the other parent is, after all, a call to take sides, and some will take the side of the family they are living with. Rebecca, Ryan's sister, needed security and a father's love. Since she felt her father Steve had left her, she forcefully took the part of her stepfather, Tim, in an effort to make sure he wouldn't leave too. Not only did she insist on calling him Dad, she resolved to tell her father she never wanted to see him again. If she had gone through with that intention, the chances are she would have bitterly regretted it and felt terrible guilt and loss.

This is why it's so important to have out whatever you feel with the other parent or the natural parent face to face, not to find fault in front of the children. The quarrel you have over unfinished business is between the adults concerned. Too often it continues to be played out in ways that hurt the children, or indeed through the children themselves. It's hardly fair to argue over access and make it difficult, as many separated parents do, when your real message is 'I'm hurt because I now think our relationship was a sham. The way you ended it left me feeling you never loved me.' If that is how you really feel, say so. Don't mess around with access in order to hurt your ex, as a way of saying it. You may have your revenge in hurting them. But in the process, you also severely damage the people you both care about most of all; your children. What will help you, your children and the person you're angry with is to talk, and to listen.

If you have **continuing conflict** with an ex you may need to think carefully whether your anger actually belongs to your ex or partner's ex, or really belongs to someone else in your own life. This is because sometimes the anger, the unfinished business and baggage, has far deeper roots than simply the former relationship and its ending. When I counselled Tim he erupted with a heartfelt outburst against his stepson Ryan's father, saying he hated him – simply hated him. He said this was because he felt Steve wasn't there for his own son, having had a period after the break-up when he neglected his own kids, spending his energy and time on his new girlfriend's children.

Active Listening

When we're upset or have a problem, talking to someone can be helpful if we feel they care and understand what we are saying. If the other person isn't paying attention, jumps in with quick fixes, tells us it's our fault or tries to brush off our concerns, it can make us feel worse.

What makes the difference is active listening. Active listening is when the other person shows they're really listening, wanting to understand and help without taking over. When you're listening, you:

- Care for, trust and accept the other person and their feelings, want to understand but don't want to sort it out for them.
- Concentrate on this person and this problem, NOW.
- Use your body – leaning forward, facing them – to show you're paying attention.
- Ask open questions – 'So, tell me about it.'
- Check out what's been said – 'Have I got this right ...?'
- Acknowledge feelings – 'That must feel hurtful.'
- Identify needs – 'What you want is ...'
- Move them on – 'So what can we do to make this better?'

Your AIM when you are listening is to:

- Acknowledge feelings – 'I can see you're angry with me.'
- Identify needs – 'You wanted to be able to stay with your Dad and we made other arrangements.'
- Move on – 'What can we do to satisfy both of us?'

Sometimes, just acknowledging feelings and needs is enough; other times the person who is talking may want to think about how they are going to sort out the problem. Be guided by them – your role as listener is to offer care and understanding, not come up with a solution.

Even now, said Tim, he never rang to see how Ryan or his sister Rebecca were doing in between the times he saw them. Tim felt this was neglectful parenting and he felt he should be left alone to be a better father to them. What emerged was that Tim had had a particularly sad childhood, with a stepfather who he felt hadn't supported him and had forbidden him to see his own father. Tim also believed his stepdad had prevented him doing things he loved such as playing football, and had not been gentle with him. Tim had an overwhelming need to be a good stepdad. He had promised himself he would never hit or ill-treat Ryan, and was offended that Ryan didn't seem to recognize this. But the key was that Tim felt utterly inhibited not only in letting his stepfather know how angry and let down he felt, but in even admitting to himself how enraged and bitterly disappointed he was about this relationship. He found it even harder to admit how let down he had felt by his mother, who hadn't sufficiently protected him from her husband. But he felt no such inhibitions at letting the anger out to be directed at Steve. So all of his rage at his stepfather and his mother went that way. Which was all very well, but for two important things. One is, as already mentioned, that when you express anger at a parent, the child feels it too. Even if you think you speak your mind at times when they don't hear, be sure they will know. Some children react with defensiveness and equal rage – Ryan and Tim had frequent rows over this, and other matters. Ryan felt Tim's criticism of his father as criticism of himself too. Some children react by rolling over – Rebecca became her new daddy's little girl, doing all she could to make Tim happy. Rather than take on Tim's criticism of Steve as anything to do with her, she rejected Steve.

Young people often find it easier to show their anger and pain in a roundabout way rather than straight on. They 'act out' their distress in various ways instead of coming at it directly. This may be because they themselves find it hard to put a finger on exactly what they are feeling. Anger can be confused with pain, disappointment with guilt and the young person may be at a loss to put a name to it. Or, they may believe – as Ryan did – that saying what he felt would be far too discomforting for him or painful for his mother to have put into words. Instead, he frequently worked himself up into punishing rants that actually hurt him, his mum and the whole family far more than sitting down and having an honest if painful discussion about what was really bothering him. This is the way young people often react – saving up their feelings until they burst out in a tantrum or rage that is far more destructive than speaking plainly and truthfully. The key change came in Ryan's family when he and his mother did sit down and calmly said what was on each other's minds, and each really heard it.

The other reason that **being angry with the wrong person**, or expressing your rage at them, is harmful to a stepfamily is that it doesn't work. If what you really need to do is finally lay to rest your anger at your own parent or stepparent, expressing it to someone else may let off steam but only for a short time, because you haven't done the real job; you haven't let the person you want to sound off at know what you feel. That nagging feeling that there is unfinished business will keep coming back. Anger will keep welling up at the wrong person, because it hasn't been expressed to the right one. What helped Tim was addressing what he really felt, for the person he really felt it about. He felt unable to actually face his stepfather and say it, or even to write to him. It can help to make the effort to do this, however difficult and painful, but sometimes this isn't possible – you can't manage it or, indeed, they won't allow it, or they may not even be around to hear it. In such cases, it can often help to do it in fantasy. You can set up a cushion on a chair and imagine they're sitting there, hearing you tell them exactly what you think. Or you can write it down, as Tim did. He did find it possible to write down everything he wanted to say, and just doing so – seeing it all down on paper – helped.

'I' Statements

When we're finding it difficult to talk things through, it might be because of the way we're putting it. It could help to use an 'I' statement. 'I' statements are all about being able to say what 'I want' and what 'I need'. They help the person speaking, and the person being spoken to, to be clear about what is really going on.

When we use an 'I' statement, we can:

- Be aware of our own feelings about what we want.

- Stand up and be counted about our feelings and needs.

- Help other people understand what we are saying.

- Be clear, honest and direct.

- Make our point without blaming, criticizing or judging other people.

When we're upset we sometimes blame the other person for what has happened: 'Look what you made me do' or 'You make me so angry!' Or we try to avoid taking responsibility for angry or critical remarks by saying they belong to someone else: 'Everyone thinks it's your fault.'

These are 'You' statements, and they seldom give the other person a chance to understand what we're upset about, how we feel or why, or give them an opportunity to make any changes. 'You' statements may be a way of not being overwhelmed by anger or despair. Instead of 'owning' feelings, we hold them at arm's length: 'One feels like that, doesn't one?'; 'That's how you do it, don't you?'

Using an 'I' statement respects the other person and their point of view. It helps you say what you feel and want but avoids making the other person feel like the problem. This makes it far easier for them to come up with a solution, take responsibility and act positively.

It can take some time to get into the habit of using 'I' statements, which isn't surprising. Most of us have had a lifetime of being told it's selfish or big-headed to say 'I'. But the more you use them, the more you'll find they work and help you and the other person feel good about the exchange.

An 'I' statement:

● Describes the behaviour I'm finding difficult.

● Says the effect it has on me.

● Tells the other person how I feel about it.

● Invites them to join me in finding a solution.

A useful formula to use is to say:

● When you … (say exactly what they are doing).

● I feel … (describe your emotions).

● Because … (say what happens).

● What I'd like is … (or What can we do about it?).

Some people find it helps, having written it down, to then burn or bury the letter. Others keep it as a way of knowing that they finally said what needed to be said.

The fact is that some of the baggage and unfinished business we carry into stepfamilies has less to do with a previous, fairly recent, relationship than it does with **shadows from the past**. Sometimes you can have a situation where stepparent and stepchild do not get on, and it's simply a case of clashing personalities. After all, you grow up with your own children and however separate and individual they may be, they are still yours and are people you develop along with as they grow up. With a stepchild, it can be a challenge because you are taking on an individual already formed and often in a mould you find unfamiliar and even unsympathetic. Chris felt he and his stepdaughter Kat clashed because they simply didn't understand each other's sense of humour. He, after all, had inherited a 10-year-old with an already well-developed character and patter when it came to jokes. She found herself with a man with attitudes and an idea of what was funny that she had to get to know. This mismatch can be particularly difficult when the child's character reminds you or your partner of their parent.

Frequently that clash is more about what the child represents to the adult, and vice versa, than their real personality. Sharon found her new partner's son Josh annoyed her. He was a 'pain in the bum', she said – she insisted he was rough with her 3-year-old daughter Rhiannon, gave her dirty looks and ignored her. She said she just couldn't get on with him, but it was up to Josh to behave better and then she'd respond. To the adult, it may be that the child is proof that there was someone there before them, with the person they love, that hurts. To the child, the new adult is the nail in the coffin to any hopes they have of their original family getting back together. The new adult supplants for good their other parent. Jealousy, resentment and anger fuel opposition. This is familiar stepfamily stuff – the normal currency of the difficulties many stepfamilies experience. But sometimes, **deeper issues** are surfacing. The adult may have real shadows in their past – early abuse, later exploitation, loss and hurt – and this can make them take out their anger or guilt or loss or confusion unfairly on the child. They may be angry at a father for having abused them, a brother for having misused them or a child for having deserted them by dying. The stepchild becomes the lightning rod for these feelings, and is a scapegoat and whipping person.

My belief was that Sharon's feelings towards Andy's son Josh were more about her own shadows than anything the child himself had done, or did – although the pressure he was under in the family meant his behaviour had changed and for the worse. Sharon had suffered sexual abuse during her childhood and had lost two children by stillbirth and two by miscarriage. Her stepson Josh was a similar age and in the same family situation – of an age between her living son, 11-year-old Josh and her 3-year-old daughter Rhiannon – to one of her dead sons, Samuel. As it happened, Sharon had chosen to link up with a man who had two children who completed her family of four. Sharon would have had a son of 15, a son of 11, a son of 6 and a daughter of 3. By moving in with Andy, she had taken on a daughter and a son slotting in to the two missing places. I don't think that this was a coincidence. We often choose partners – and, in stepfamilies, their family – who 'fit in' with needs that we may not have recognized or realized. Sharon had been drawn to someone whose family could complete her and fill in her loss. But, having got him and his children, she found herself feeling angry and resentful towards one of these children. Not Andy's daughter Sian, who didn't exactly rival the missing, dead Liam, but Josh, who was in Samuel's place and wasn't Samuel. As with many people in similar situations, when Sharon felt angry, she shouted. She said it made her feel strong and so she found it impossible to stop. Indeed, since she thought it made her feel better, she was resistant to the idea of stopping at first. And she shouted at Josh, because he was there and in the position to take her blame. In some families there is a sense of helplessness and hopelessness – the situation seems so complex and fraught, so involved and difficult, that everyone reaches a point where there seems to be no way back.

Sometimes the baggage you carry with you that might affect your stepfamily can be from the distant past, the recent past or a combination. It's always worth asking yourself 'What happened around then?' when things start going wrong. However well they may seem to be weathering it, coming into a stepfamily is an obvious trigger to set children off in what seems to be bad behaviour. It isn't them being bad; it's them expressing bad, unhappy, confused feelings in the only way they know how. But you may also ask yourself what happened to set you off, too. Don't forget that your family has something painful, something associated with loss and pain, guilt and anger, in its very foundation. Roby and Anne Marie found themselves arguing bitterly a few months after she moved in with him and his three children. They couldn't understand why this was happening. Anne Marie had met Roby two years after his wife had died, and his children had made her welcome and the two of them got on really well until that point. It wasn't until they realized the tension had flared up on the anniversary of his wife's death – the first year Anne Marie had been living with them since her death – that they recognized it as his guilt and confusion, and lingering grief.

For Chris and Tracie, it was something that happened in the first year of their relationship that cast a pall. One thing all Chris's stepchildren seemed to agree on was that he seemed nice at first, when he came to live with them. He was fun, and he and their mother Tracie were happy together, and they all appreciated that he did her good. But then, they said, after a year, he became

Talking by Timer

There's another technique I used in the TV series, one that many families found particularly useful and that anyone can do. This was using a one-minute egg-timer to set up a listening and talking exercise between two people. We often find it hard to say what we really mean to someone else, whether it's telling them about the day-to-day trivia of what happened to us today, or telling them something really important about our needs or anxieties. It's often hard because we fear we'll be interrupted or the other person won't be listening. And hearing what another person is trying to tell us is just as hard – we often don't take the time or make the effort to tune in.

You can use the timer to start talking and listening between you. Toss a coin for who will go first. The first person sets the timer going and has 1 minute to talk, WITHOUT INTERRUPTION. Their job is to say exactly what they want or need to say to the other person. The job of the listener is to do that, and that only. The listener should show, with active listening – leaning forward, making eye contact, nodding and saying 'Uh huh' that they are paying attention, but they can't interrupt or comment on what they are hearing. After the set amount of time, change roles. The new speaker shouldn't use the opportunity to simply come back and argue with what they've just heard – they should say something they'd already planned to speak about.

Once you've done it a few times you may like to extend the time. You may also decide to move on to discussing things using the Active Listening skills that using the egg-timer helps you develop.

bad-tempered and 'a monster'. They couldn't understand why – maybe it was their fault: 'Maybe we stopped making an effort and that's why it all went wrong.' When I spoke with Chris and Tracie, they mentioned, almost in passing, that there had been a miscarriage a few months before their first child was conceived. This pregnancy had been difficult and they hadn't known if the baby would survive. Oh – and they hadn't told the kids about the miscarriage, because they thought it would upset them. What neither Chris nor Tracie had quite understood was the effect the miscarriage had had on themselves – especially on Chris, for whom this would have been a first child. He had been devastated – as he put it, gutted. He became depressed. But he also felt guilty, thinking as many people do in such a situation, that somehow the miscarriage was his fault and divine retribution for past sins. This feeling of guilt resulted in simmering anger – at the world and at himself. They may have kept the children from the reason for his behaviour but they couldn't protect them from the behaviour itself – his constant, seething fury and resentment, which resulted in a short fuse and frequent outbursts. When Chris and Tracie were able to consider, 'What happened around then?' and see the connection, Chris felt as if a weight had been lifted from his shoulders. He said he got up the next day realizing it was the first morning in three years that he hadn't woken up angry. And he was able to begin to mend bridges with Tracie's children – not least, by telling them what had happened, what he'd felt and why, and apologizing for keeping them in the dark and for his behaviour. They responded with understanding and sympathy – although they did quite rightly ask, 'Why didn't you tell us then?' The answer was that he hadn't been able to put his feelings into words, it was too close and too raw perhaps for him to examine it. And, like so many people in similar situations, he really hadn't realized how much the event had affected them, and how his behaviour would affect the kids. And he and Tracie really had believed they were doing the right thing. The message to anyone in such a situation is to ask the question, and communicate.

Some stepfamily problems are about being in a stepfamily. It's about getting to know children who are not your own, or helping a new partner do so. It's about dealing with the unfinished business left over from past relationships, about **taking on a package deal** of someone else's children. But nobody comes into a family with a totally clean sheet. You're a parent or stepparent on the foundation of having been in a family – your family of origin. You learn how to be a parent from your own mum and dad, and the things you saw, felt and experienced taught you about loving, caring for and being cared for – or not. If you were treated with sympathy and empathy, respect and love, you are likely to have taken such skills on board and be able to show them to others. If your experience of being parented left you feeling uncared for, unheard, unworthy, you are likely to find it hard to care, to listen or to make others feel worthwhile. From the age of 11, Ade had been the 'bad boy' of his family, bullied by his father, not defended by his mother and eventually spent time in care. He was finding it hard to relate to his stepson Daniel, when he finally got confirmation of something he had suspected for years – that his father was actually his stepfather. Having lied about it for years, his parents simply refused to talk about it. Stepfamily partnerships have that extra layer; not only what you learnt from your parents and the experience of being a child, but also what your past relationships taught you about putting it together as an adult. Whatever you carried over from your childhood that might have contributed to a difficulty in making and keeping a relationship, and which might have contributed to the breakdown of your first relationship, will still be there. Added may be a sense of failure and guilt about the way the first family – and any subsequent ones – broke up.

All families have difficulties. When toddlers have tantrums or teenagers 'kick off' in a stepfamily, it may be hard to tell whether it's about missing a parent who doesn't live with you or getting used to a new partner, or whether it's simply normal toddler or teenage stuff. Always remind yourself, it could be about toddlers finding their voice or teenagers attempting to stand on their own two feet and separate from their parents. You may find it easier to blame the special situation of your family to explain it rather than accept that all teens and all toddlers can clash with their parents at times. They in turn may find it to their advantage to make a point, and make you feel guilty, by playing the stepfamily card when it's nothing to do with that.

If you're struggling to come to terms with something such as an abusive past, being in a stepfamily can ramp up the problems. You can't put all the blame and all the anxiety on being in a stepfamily – it may be some of that unfinished business or baggage that's actually to blame. Anna, like many stepparents, puts much of the blame for conflicts in her stepfamily on one child, in her case her stepdaughter Gita. Her behaviour to Gita is extreme, constantly shouting at her and encouraging Gita's brother and her own son to blame Gita for any quarrels or disagreements in the family. Anna was sexually abused by her own father, and because of her early experiences she appears to be entirely lacking in the ability to empathize or even sympathize. After all, if no one has ever showed you empathy or sympathy these are skills you may not develop. Her mother refused to believe her when she asked for help, and indeed blamed Anna herself for anything that might be happening or have happened – she made it clear she didn't want to hear details. If one of you or both of you come from families that leave you lacking in self-esteem – with parents who leave you feeling unworthy, who let you down or betray you in some way – that has an echo in your ability to parent.

The problem with trying to ignore the baggage and unfinished business from your past is that it doesn't disappear. Instead, the more you try to brush

Genograms

Help yourself to see the ways your past may be affecting you by doing a Genogram – a sort of family tree. Traditional family trees simply show who is there and related to whom. Stepfamily trees may be more complex because you have to take into account people who aren't blood-linked to you but are important nonetheless. Genograms do much more – they can show you why your family, you and your partner are the way you are, and give you clues to how you may change the things you don't like.

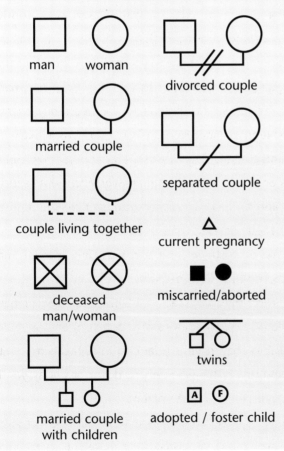

man   woman

divorced couple

married couple

separated couple

couple living together

current pregnancy

deceased man/woman

miscarried/aborted

twins

married couple with children

adopted / foster child

Sit down with a large piece of paper and draw a map of your family. Use the symbols shown here.

Put yourself and your partner at the centre of the page and draw in your parents and siblings, ex-partners and children. Note beside each person a small 'word drawing' of them – the things that spring to mind about each person, that you can remember or have heard. Be honest.

Look for repeating patterns in your own family. Look for things that come up on both your and your partner's side, or are dramatically different. Look for events that might have some bearing on why you or your partner or your children may feel certain things, behave in certain ways.

Stephen and Pauline's Genogram

When Stephen and Pauline came for help with their stepfamily, they did a Genogram to help them look at what might be happening.

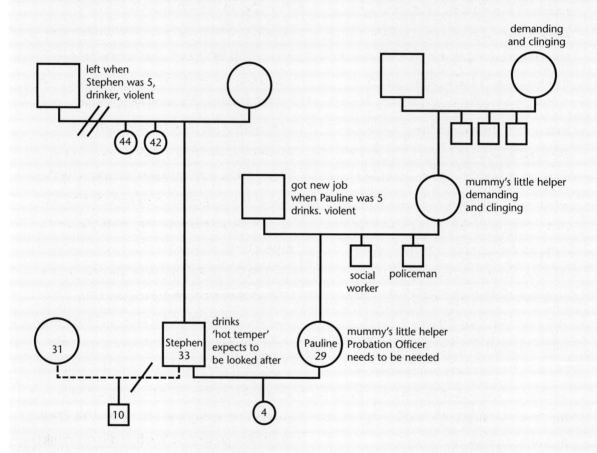

Their daughter was now 4, and Pauline was worried about the way their relationship seemed to have deteriorated over the past year. Stephen drank too much, and while not exactly violent he could be 'over the top' when he had too much. He hardly saw his own son, saying it was too difficult to keep the relationship together – he and his ex had parted when the boy was 5.

What emerged from the Genogram was that both of them had fathers who were alcoholic and abusive and had gone absent when they were 5 – Stephen's father left, and Pauline's got a new job that took him away a lot. Pauline had been her mother's 'little helper', expected to look after her younger siblings. Her grandmother, who also lived with them, was very demanding and a lot less feeble than she let on. Pauline's mother had also had to look after her siblings when she was young. On Stephen's side, his sisters were teenagers at the time their father left and he says it was probably their fault.

So Pauline and Stephen have in common drinking fathers who left the scene – a scenario Stephen has already repeated once. Pauline and her siblings take care of people – a legacy bequeathed by their mother and grandmother. Stephen is the baby of his family who takes it for granted women will look after him. Pauline is driven to find someone who needs to be looked after and rescued, someone who drinks and ignores his family, and to try to change him into the loving, kind father who stays. Both assume that women not only have to look after everyone, but take the blame when it goes wrong. With their daughter approaching the age of 5, if Stephen and Pauline didn't look at their family patterns, they might be set to repeat them.

What they both did with the help of the Genogram was examine the situation – looking at their shared legacy, and the beliefs that went with it. Stephen got help with his drinking and started taking some responsibility for his own feelings; Pauline stopped assuming she had to do it all. They are still together and Stephen doesn't drink any more – their daughter is in secondary school and Stephen's son visits regularly.

stuff under the carpet, the more it will trip you up. You do need to **identify your baggage**, have it out and deal with it in order to be able to put it aside. Tim not only faced up to his anger with his stepfather, he also took on board the fact that some of his anger at his stepchildren's father, Steve, for not being as hands-on a dad as Tim thought he should be, was actually his own guilt speaking. Tim had a son of his own, the same age as Ryan and even in Ryan's class at school, whom he had not seen since he was a baby. But most admirable of all, Tim and Steve decided to address their disagreements in a face-to-face talk. The main problem in such situations is that both parties so often stereotype the other's reactions or behaviour or reasons. They need someone to blame and so create a cartoon 'bad person' in their mind and insist that's what the other is. In Tim and Steve's case, a few of their friends and relatives stirred the situation just before they met, spreading rumours that Steve only wanted to have the meeting as an excuse to get Tim in a room and hit him. Nothing could be further from the truth – Steve certainly wanted and needed the opportunity to tell Tim about his anger, and to know that Tim had heard it, but violence wasn't on the cards. Tim had the courage and decency to trust that a face-to-face meeting was going to remain civilized. Both of them came out of the meeting feeling they had gained understanding and a resolution.

Whether your last family ended with confrontations or sadness, whether the relationship was a long or short one, if you have separated badly you owe it to yourself and your children – and indeed your ex and any new partner – to try to redress that now. Like Lynn and Steve, you might use a mediator or a counsellor to have a last 'wrap up' meeting to say what needs to be said, in an atmosphere where hurt can be managed and contained, and left behind. You can agree to be parents forever, even though being a partner can end. It's worth remembering that the courts would far rather you sorted out between you how you are going to manage access and living arrangements for your children. They prefer only to get involved if you can't agree. Rather than waste time, effort and money – and indeed force all of you into a confrontation – it's best to consent between you how you will settle it and go forward. And however much you may think getting all the people concerned round a table sounds impossible, it really does help if both original parents and stepparents – all the people who will share the task of caring for these children – get together to talk about it and see eye-to-eye.

Asking for support from mediation or counselling can make a difference. You then get an objective reassessment of what has happened, and help in seeing the situation from everyone's point of view. Above all, don't allow other people such as family members or friends to stir up trouble. When Matt had an affair with his wife Donna's best friend, a mutual friend of theirs suggested she should take him for every penny he had and absolutely refuse to let him see their children. 'After all,' she said, 'do you want her bringing up your kids?' Donna's new partner Paul also felt angry at Matt, criticizing him as a bad father for what he had done. Donna saw a counsellor, who helped her and Matt talk. She was angry at him but recognized that however badly he had treated her, he did desperately want to be a good father to his son, and she made it as easy as possible for him to go on seeing the boy. She also insisted that her friends and family respect him as a father and help her in this; her first rule was never, ever, on pain of being banned from seeing their son, to criticize Matt in front of him. It doesn't matter what other people feel about your break-up or the new family or what they do in their own lives – you can decide to behave well.

Casting an honest eye over your unfinished business and baggage helps you come to terms with the past but also helps you insure your future. Even if you feel you were the innocent party, it pays to consider what you might have done or not done that contributed to the break-up, and what you might want to change now. You have a choice about your past. Some people try to deny it – to insist everything that happened was another person's fault and they are victims. Or they try to edit it, rewriting in their minds or in the story they tell others to make themselves feel better. Or they try to forget elements or the significance of some parts of their history. None of this is helpful. Your relationship with an ex may be over, but seeing it as a mistake or as something that never mattered may seem to help you get over the pain of an ending, but it doesn't. For a start, how can you trust yourself and your instincts and feelings if you lie to yourself about something as important as that? And how will your children feel, to hear or learn or gather that they are part of a mistake and something you regret? The best way to deal with all that unfinished business and baggage is to accept it and deal with it. You may need to finish some of it – to go back and have your say either face-to-face, and listen in return, or to do it in fantasy. You may need help and support to face up to some destructive, painful elements such as abuse or conflict. You can get it, either from friends and family or professionals such as mediators or counsellors. You can access such help from your own family doctor, or through some of the organizations I list at the end of this book. All in all, you owe it to yourself and your family to deal with whatever is behind you, in order to fully enjoy and develop the family you and your children and your partner now want to be.

Some Things to Keep in Mind

- However a family ends, you'll always be left with unfinished business – be prepared to deal with this as soon as you can.

- Unfinished business or baggage will not disappear if ignored. Brushing stuff under the carpet simply forms a bump you'll keep tripping over.

- It often helps to have a final 'wrap up' meeting with your ex to say what you need to say and hear what you need to hear, to finally put the past to rest. Then you can get on with discussing and agreeing how you are going to co-parent your children.

- A mediator or counsellor would be particularly helpful to guide the discussion and keep it from getting out of control. Don't let embarrassment get in the way of asking for help.

- Get your anger and anxieties about your ex into perspective. Someone only has power over you if you give it. Don't let anger that properly belongs in the past spoil either your new relationship or your, your partner's or the other parent's relationship with the children.

- You may want a total split from an ex. Children want and need continuing contact with both parents. Balancing these apparently conflicting needs is the key to a happy stepfamily.

Chapter 4

Different Agendas

Adults and children in a stepfamily have a very different view of what is going on. For a start, it is the adults who make all the decisions – to end one relationship, and to begin another. It is the adults who are in charge of leaving one family unit and forming a new one. The adults concerned may feel powerless and out of control of their lives and that what is going on may simply be fate or 'something that just happens'. Indeed, the original separation or the new stepfamily could have come about because of the decision of another adult. But however much adults may consider they are in the grip of forces beyond their control, this is nothing to how the children are likely to feel. Feeling swept along by passion or anger is not the same as coming home one day to have your father tell you he is leaving and thinks it best if he doesn't see you again. Or your mother tell you Tom, Dick or Harry is moving in with his children Janet and John and you have to share your room. Now, that is being out of control and powerless. Some adults may go through the motions of telling their children in advance, and even asking their opinion or permission. In reality, children have no say and know it.

Who makes the choice to break and make a family is not the least of the differences in the way adults and children perceive stepfamilies. Another major difference is the place the parent who leaves occupies in the lives of their ex, and their children. For an adult breaking up with a partner it is the end of a relationship that occupied part of their life. You might have felt your partner was the most important and central aspect – the foundation of your happiness and your family. Still, even if he or she was a childhood friend, you will remember a time before you knew them. They may be important in your life but they aren't critical. If you're the child, your parent seems to be a fixture. They were there, after all, before you were. As far back as you can remember, they were around – a permanent part of your life and the building block on which everything else is based. In ending a relationship with a partner, an adult returns to the way they might have been previous to the relationship, knowing they existed and managed before their partner came on the scene. However badly you may feel during the break-up, fundamentally you realize, or will come to realize, you can still exist without them. Children simply may not have that understanding. With a parent gone, their entire world view shifts and becomes insecure and frightening. They may not be able to see how they can manage, because they never have.

On top of such a loss, if one or both of their parents start **new relationships** this can feel even more upsetting instead of seeming helpful. When a new family comes along, children and adults have this essential difference. For the adults at the centre of a new family it is a new beginning. Even if the break-up was another adult's choice, the start of the new family is theirs, and they can feel good about that. Most of all, it is the launch of something exciting, hopeful and joyful. It is a beginning: of an adventure, a whole new life, another chance. Most adults will feel hopeful, glad, optimistic, excited. They will be looking forward, wanting to sweep away the sadness that may have dragged them down before and to put behind them a past that seems full of mistakes, false starts and failures.

For the children, and the left-behind adult, it is often a calamity. Above all, what is a beginning for you is an ending for them. Some children may not be quite as negative or sad about the ending of their old family as others, and some may not be as hostile towards the new family either. If there have been continued arguments and prolonged misery, especially if verbal, emotional or even physical violence was threatened or present, children as well as adults may be relieved at having the birth parents call an end to it. They may find more support and kindness from the stepparent than from their own, or be delighted in their parent's happiness. But even if on one level they rejoice at the new regime, children still feel the new relationship is the final nail in the coffin of the old family and many of their hopes. Even beyond reason, for months if not years, children will cling to the fantasy that their 'own', 'real' family may come back together again. Come back in a better shape, with the arguments resolved and the people concerned happy and getting on. When a new person takes the place of the missing parent, those hopes may be dashed. If the stepparent and parent then announce they plan to make their relationship permanent, either by marrying or getting a home together, children may have a profound sense of loss. This will be a loss of their dreams, their hopes and expectations, however unrealistic, and it can lead to depression or moodiness, or the acting out of bad feelings in bad behaviour. Children may get caught up in the excitement of the new arrangements, especially new homes or weddings, but at the same time show feelings they themselves may not realize they have in arguments with the adults, spats among themselves or rebellion. Fifteen-year-old Amy, 12-year-old Vicky and 11-year-old Sam got on badly with their stepdad, Ian. He and their mother,

Denise, had married in Gretna Green seventeen weeks after meeting – without telling the children what they had planned. Amy, Vicky and Sam had more losses to cope with than most children. Amy and Vicky's father, Darren, left when Denise was pregnant with Vicky. Sam's dad, Andy, left when she was little. Even Denise's parents, their grandparents, decamped to Portugal and cut off all contact. Amy reacted by bossing and looking after everyone, Vicky by being a determined joker, and Sam by crying often.

The fact that people in the same family will see the same event in such a different light is at the heart of most stepfamily difficulties. Adults may be at

Giving in Fantasy

Parents often believe that if their child wants or feels something different to them, and they accept and take their feelings on board, this will lead to problems. Maybe they will see this as a weakness and take advantage. Or maybe by admitting to the possibility of difference you create it. Neither is true. Your children will have their feelings whether you admit to them or not. What they may not be able to do if those feelings are denied is deal with them. Let's take the case of a child who misses their father and wishes you would leave your new partner get back with him. You could tell the child, 'You like Nick, don't you? You're happy with Nick, aren't you? You know I don't love your dad any more and he made Mummy sad? You don't want Mummy to be sad, do you? You're happy here, aren't you?'

What would you expect the child to say? 'Yes, I want to make Mummy miserable?' Of course not; they'll sulk and mutter, or dutifully agree that they want Mummy happy and they are happy. Their feelings won't go away, though. They'll come out in other ways – in depression, naughtiness or self-harm. It's very tempting as parents to want to reassure – to try to carry on as if everything is fine. By insisting it is so, we a loss to see why their children are being so contrary and badly behaved. With minds focused on the upside of it all, it feels quite a wrench, and an irritating one at that, to have children pulling in the opposite direction. You may find yourself quick to be angry and cast blame for what you see as bloody-mindedness. It might seem so simple to you; the original relationship didn't work out, and this new one will. There were rows and sadness before and now you have the chance to make it better. Who wouldn't want to try to make an effort? Sharon, for instance, would insist that she was happy in her new relationship with Andy and their shared

hope to carry through what we want by asserting it is. But insisting that you are happy or they are or should be happy doesn't make it so simply because you say so. Kids aren't stupid – they know when you aren't being real. All this does is make them doubt their own instincts, senses and intelligence, or distrust you.

Try another tack. Why not say, 'I'm really sad you're missing your dad. He and I don't get on as we did and we can't live together any more. But he's your dad and I know you love him and he loves and misses you. We both love you the same as we ever did. I wish I could make it better for you, somehow. What would help?'

Your child may want more contact – not just face to face, but in texts and calls and emails. They may also want to have photos of the birth dad and original family easily available and on show. Above all, your child needs to hear you say that you hear, understand, allow and accept their feelings, however different they may be to yours. Just knowing this makes an immense difference to them. And while you may find it painful to have to accept that they have a different view to you – still loving, perhaps forgiving and certainly needing as a parent the partner you no longer have – it won't hurt you as much as having to bow to your agenda will hurt them.

home together. Yes, it wasn't ideal, as they only had three bedrooms and her children had to share a room, and Andy's two had to share one too. And she knew that her son missed his father and wanted more contact. But she believed her son Josh needed to know she would never go back to his father and that was the end of it. 'He can't have what he wants so there's no point in talking about it,' she said. 'I'm happy, so you should be happy too. You're happy, aren't you?' Put on the spot like that, children find it very hard to voice their concerns and true feelings, and so are often left feeling guilty and to blame as well as sad. Just because you can't or won't do as they would choose does not mean you should or can insist your children feel the same way as you do about the situation.

Children may not be able to understand why a parent is so set on doing something that seems so manifestly cruel or unfair. You are discarding their parent. Even if it was the other parent who left and made that choice, children often feel safer in blaming the one who's left behind. If you are the one moving into a stepfamily, you will certainly get it in the neck from your children for foisting strangers upon them. Even if what they actually find in the family suits them, they still may resist – more about that in Chapter 7: Family Structures. Gaining a new baby, a younger brother or sister to boss around, an older one to look up to or a same-age sibling to become a good friend, may be fun. It still spells a change to their original family, one they might view with suspicion and resentment. It's easy to recognize that everyone loses out and has something to mourn when a family breaks up. It's less easy to see that while, for you, much of what happens in the establishment of a stepfamily will be a gain, it may yet again be seen by the children as loss.

When Sharon and Andy got together, for instance, they each gained a partner, hope and love. For their children it was less simple. Her son, 11-year-old Josh, for instance, lost:

- his original family
- his father – he still sees him but that's not the same as living with him
- his home – they moved some distance to live with Andy and his two children
- his school
- his local friends
- his own room – in the new home, he had to share with his 3-year-old sister
- and even sole rights to his own name, as Andy's 9-year-old son was coincidently also called Josh

This Josh, having earlier lost:

- his mother – he still sees her regularly but that's not the same as living with her
- his original family

has now lost:

- his own room – he had to move in with his 13-year-old sister
- his own family, as three new people moved in
- his place in the family, as he was no longer the youngest
- time with his Dad, who now had four children to care for
- a good relationship with his sister, who now sided with the older Josh
- sole rights to his own name

A **move away** from one area to another, from one home to another, can mean inspiring and exciting forward-looking change for the adults. You see it as a fresh start, leaving behind bad memories and connections you'd rather forget. It may be hard to recognize just how much your children may lose rather than gain in such a move – friends, contacts, memories, a sense of belonging and knowing exactly where they stand and who they are. It may be an important strategy in order to help the new family work for you all to begin again, in a new home or at least in a newly arranged house. But you do need to at least recognize and be able to admit to the children that this involves a loss to them as well.

A stepparent may look upon the new family as a **second chance** at being a good parent. They may see the opportunity to succeed in the parenting stakes with other people's children as they may not have been able to do with their own. When Ali married Sonia, he was determined to love and support her two sons and to do his best as a stepfather. He had left his former wife when his son was 11 and his daughter 14, and the fact that he had concentrated more on his career than his family meant that he and they had rapidly lost touch. He and Sonia's sons soon formed a strong and loving bond and it made him re-examine the way he had fathered his own children, and the way he might be with them now. When he heard his daughter was to be married, he got in touch. At first, she was hostile and rejected his attempts at contact. He eventually asked her to see him with a counsellor, and she eventually gave in. He told her how sorry he was at failing her and how much he would like to make up for it, accepting that it might be too late and that he felt that was all his own fault. Being able to express her anger and disappointment in him meant she was then able to move through it, and both she and her brother eventually made up with him. The experience of having a stepfamily he enjoyed had played a part in allowing Ali to go back and make up in some ways for the way he had let down his children earlier.

This doesn't always work, of course. Stepchildren may heartily resent any efforts at your shining up your own image through them. And your own, left-behind children may be equally resentful and disinclined to play your scenario. You can't put children on hold, hoping to go back and mend your ways and your relationship with them later. Lee had children by two previous partners before he met Carly. Both relationships had ended bitterly, and both mothers refused to let Lee see his children. Lee believed that he would be able to reunite with his children when they were older and could make their own decisions to see him, and make their own minds up about what had driven him and their mothers apart. Until he met Carly, he was convinced that he had always been the victim and his kids would see that. When he had the chance to think this through with her help, he realized that there were faults on both sides in the break-up, and that his failings as a father were his own responsibility. He also recognized that it was most likely that while his children might once have wanted to have contact with him, they might also have had too long away from him. If their main image of him was of the man who abandoned and thus rejected them, they might be unable to remake the relationship.

Nor can you rewrite your own history by being a good parent to your stepchildren. Tony had had a poor relationship with his stepfather, who prevented him seeing his own dad and was unsupportive and unpredictable. Part of Tony's resolve to be a good stepfather to his stepson Brian was a desire, of which he was unaware, to somehow make it better for himself. Somewhere in Tony was the belief that if he could be a loving and loved stepfather for Brian, it would be as if his own stepfather had done the right thing by him too. Of course, it never works that way. If such unconscious wishes are what drives you, you are doomed to feel unsatisfied and cheated. Not least because the children concerned, who have no such wishes and can't understand yours, won't play ball, as their needs may run counter to yours. Tony, for instance, desperately needed Brian to choose him above his own father, and to acknowledge how much better Tony was than his own stepfather in that he never raised a hand to Brian, while his own stepfather had been violent. Brian, however, needed to remain in close contact with his own father, Simon, and had no intention of making a choice between them and didn't realize that Tony not hitting him was anything to acknowledge.

Of course, in some stepfamilies the **different agendas** adults and children may have could involve the very existence of the children. In some cases the stepparent takes on a partner with children, but actually only focuses on the adult. What they want is a relationship with their new partner, and as far as they are concerned the children may come too, but that's only an inconvenient detail. One adult would like them to be a family – the other only wants them to be a couple. We'll look at that in more detail in the next chapter.

As well as having different agendas to the adults in a stepfamily, children in the family can also have different agendas from each other. Children may well make their own dynamics within their own family or in the new stepfamily. They can be hostile to newcomers, or welcoming while turning against siblings they might have got on with before. They can make alliances, together against adults or as two or three ganging up on other children in the new family. One may want to cooperate with the new stepparent, as did Rebecca, and so be seen by another sibling as 'going over to the other side'. As well as losing a parent, some kids can thus also lose a sibling in the reshuffle, like Ryan, who felt his sister Rebecca no longer loved him or wasn't on his side. Caitlin's two children by different fathers – 13-year-old Tamsin and 8-year-old Jonah – had got on well until Trevor moved in. Jonah sees his own birth father regularly but Tamsin does not. Trevor in turn has his own son, Connor, over regularly. Tamsin felt the odd one out and alone in not seeing hers. Similarly, Andy's 9-year-old son, Josh, lost the warm relationship he had had with his 13-year-old sister Sian, who found a closer ally in Sharon's son Josh who, at 11, is closer in age to her and also, like her, at secondary school. When Amy and Vicky's father, Darren, got back in touch, Amy found the situation difficult and unsettling. She'd had too many losses and disappointments to be able to trust him instantly and wholeheartedly.

She and her sister Vicky were soon in opposition as Vicky refused to face up to any deep feelings about the situation or talk about them with her sister.

The different agendas issue can also come up when you look at the differing needs, expectations and wishes of adults within the stepfamily unit and those outside. The stepparent and their partner may want to make a good, strong family and part of doing this may be reinforcing your family as a unit; us against the world. When you do this, you want there to be a boundary – like a garden fence – around yourselves, keeping all of you safe and the outside world out. It may seem threatening in such a situation to have people wanting to breach those boundaries, as non-resident parents may seem to do, walking in and expecting some of your children to belong to them as well. It's as if the outsider wants to come in, and you may only feel safe if you don't let them. But members of your own family may want to let them in and it can feel as if you're under siege, with some of the defenders sneakily opening the gates behind your back. And of course, in some cases members of your family may be wanting an outsider to come and play their part and it's the one on the outside who doesn't want to, as in the case of a distant parent who refuses or can't take on responsibility for a child they have left. What may make this particularly difficult is that you may feel you have made a concession in lowering your defences in order to help the child, and you're affronted if the adult rejects your offer.

It's not only the agendas of ex-partners that may intrude on your family. Friends, relatives such as grandparents and siblings may have their own ideas of what is good for you, what may be going on, and what is good for them. Steve, the father of Ryan and Rebecca, and their stepfather Tim decided they would bite the bullet and have a meeting. The intention was to take the opportunity to have their say about what upset them in the break-up of Steve and Lynn's marriage and in the way Steve had managed being a distant father

Looking after Yourself

Being a parent or a stepparent is a really important and difficult job. You often spend all your time looking after everyone else in the family and leave yourself to last.

If you want to give your children what they need from you, it's vital that you look after your own needs too. It can be difficult and painful to give other people what they need if you feel nobody looks after you. It's like sharing a cup of tea or coffee. If your cup is empty and someone asks for a sip, you have to say, 'I'm sorry – there's nothing for me so there's nothing for you, either.' If your cup is half full, you may be able to say, 'Well, you can have some but if I give you a sip there won't be much left for me.' But if your cup is full, you can say, 'Have as much as you want!'

It's easy to be overwhelmed by your families' needs and for your cup to get emptied very quickly. If you're running on empty, you have nothing to give to yourself and nothing for the other important people in your life. This can leave you feeling worthless and useless, and all of you feeling resentful and angry.

Looking after yourself isn't being selfish. It's being aware that you're important too and deserve to be cared for just as much as anyone else. And that the better you feel, the better you can help other people feel too. You owe it to

- yourself
- your family
- the others in your life

since. Each felt angry about the other, and both hoped it would help to get it said and then move on. Then Tim was told that Steve only wanted to meet him so he could get him in a room and beat him up, which was entirely untrue. The people who said this may have been well-meaning and concerned about Tim's well-being. They may have felt they were telling Tim things he needed to hear. Or they may have enjoyed the gossips thrill of being 'in the to do things – even small things – to make yourself feel good. Every little treat helps to fill your cup so that you have got something to give out.

So how do you fill your cup?

Take some time to work out what makes you feel looked after, cared for, rested and refreshed. It might be

- having a bath
- reading a magazine
- taking a walk
- going shopping with a friend
- planning a holiday
- phoning or texting a friend
- watching a favourite TV programme
- meeting a friend for coffee
- having a meal alone with your partner

Make time

There are only so many hours in the day, but that doesn't mean you can't have some time for yourself. Often, the only reason you don't is because you feel you don't have a right to it. MAKE time by planning ahead, knowing it's essential for you and everyone else.

Be realistic

If you set your sights too high, you won't get there and then may feel you can't expect anything. Be realistic about what you want and build up from there.

Ask for help

Let other people know directly and clearly what you'd like.

know', as they saw it. It didn't help an already fraught situation, but fortunately both men rose above it and the meeting was entirely successful and helpful. It underlined the fact, though, that however much it might feel reassuring to have your own friends apparently rooting for you and on your side, their efforts may go towards making them feel good but not actually help you. A change in family may affect them as much as it affects you. You may not be as available as you once were to your friends and family during the difficult times when you are building your new stepfamily, and some of them may resent this and have their own reasons for being less helpful than you might wish. It's worth remembering that everyone has their own interests, and that the help they offer, the advice they suggest, may come with a few strings attached, before you take it.

The bottom line is that everyone has their own agenda – you and your partner, your children, your exes, your friends and relatives. You all want, need and often expect something different and it is the clash of these demands that can make stepfamilies so hard. It often isn't possible to please everyone; you have to make choices and decide priorities. Being aware of the fact that you do have different views and needs doesn't necessarily make it any easier to reconcile them. After all, they are often at total odds. You want a happy family with your children and Bob, while your two children want their father Bill back and Bob's three kids want him back with their mother. And your Mum wishes you'd married that nice Bert in the first place. But if you at least recognize that there may be a gap, and often a considerable one, you can do something about it. You have a better chance of reconciling the separate agendas when you can tease them apart. When you acknowledge that everyone wants something different, children are often very relieved. It helps to be told that you do know they have a viewpoint poles apart from yours – it means they don't have to feel guilty or wrong or resentful when they know they don't see things as you do. This gives you all the opportunity to discuss what it is you'd really like and how you can fit it together so that everyone gets at least part of what they need. And being open about the differing pressures also allows you to put some agendas firmly aside. That your sister can no longer drop in whenever she chooses and dump her kids on you to baby-sit because you now have three extra stepchildren to look after is her problem, not yours.

Things to Keep in Mind

- To the adults a stepfamily is a new beginning and the chance of a new life. To the children, it is the final end of their old, familiar life. It really helps if you can take on board that their feelings will be different to yours.

- A move to a new house, or even a new area, may unsettle you because it means new friends, new work, but it can also feel like a fresh start. Your children may only see the loss of friends, family and their support network. All of you may need special help and understanding to make the change.

- If you take on a partner who has children, you take on a family, too. Focus on them as well as the new adult in your life.

- If there are two sets of children involved, recognize that they may be struggling to manage the different viewpoints, wishes and needs all of them may have.

- Exes, relatives and the whole outside world have some call and effect on your family – talk it over with your partner how you will manage this.

- Communicate, communicate, communicate! There will be so many different needs and wishes, you're going to have to negotiate and compromise to make it work.

Chapter 5

The Package Deal

When you link up with someone with children from a previous relationship, you take on a package deal. As some computer experts say, it is a WYSIWYG situation – What You See Is What You Get. Where there are existing children you need to understand that you can't pick and choose. You can 'cherry-pick' a lot in life – that outfit with a different blouse; this car with the additional CD player; a burger without the pickle and ketchup. When it comes to families, Children Come Too. You can't expect the adult you love to come separate from their children and past entanglements or to have a relationship with you in spite of the children. It's a relationship with the children – or there's going to be trouble. Whether the children live with you or not, they are a part of your partner's life and yours, and you both have to make space for that fact. And that means you or your partner, or both of you, taking on the fact that you each have a past, a history and that some time in this history along came children. In addition, you both need to accept that this past is not dead, gone and forgotten. It reaches forward into the present and the future too, in the shape of the ex, the children's other parent, and the links this parent continues to have with them. The missing parent may not even be on the scene – their existence and their effect on the children affects you, even so.

One of the many issues that troubled Jenny and her family when she married Tom was that the father of one of her children had no contact at all with his son. Jenny had three children. The father of 13-year-old Adam and 11-year-old Sam was in regular contact with them, seeing them most weekends, at least one night a week and calling them every day. He also took 9-year-old Martin out, even though Martin was someone else's son. Martin's father had separated from Jenny after bitter arguments, and even though he lived nearby, refused to have anything to do with Jenny and Martin. Jenny thought it better not to talk about him at all, thinking that bringing up the subject would make it worse for her son. In fact, the subject of his father being a family secret only deepened Martin's misery. Sam realized he could really press Martin's buttons if he teased him about not having a father. It was as if poor Martin had a father-shaped hole in his life, and nothing would fill it. Martin liked Tom and got on well with him at first, which was probably why he gradually made him the focus of all his rage and grief over not having a 'real' dad like his brothers. It got so bad that Martin would get up and walk out of the room whenever Tom came in. Tom failed for quite some time to come to terms with what was going on, because he couldn't get his head round the fact that Martin's missing father was an issue they needed to consider and confront if they were to get anywhere with their new family.

Taking on a Package Deal may well mean having to accept the existence, needs and wishes of your stepchildren's other parent. But it also may mean having to deal with the fallout of their not being there. An invisible, non-existent parent is still a parent and has a life if only in the imagination, desires and hopes of a child. The final straw came for Tom when he bought Martin an expensive present for his tenth birthday. Martin ripped it open with excitement, but then took one look at the card that came with it and threw it into the corner the room. Tom thought he was selfish, greedy and ungrateful, and it stirred up a huge row that ended with Martin running away. When the dust had settled, it took a counsellor to uncover the enormous hurt and disappointment Martin was carrying over the fact that the present hadn't been from his father. He'd thought that going into double figures would finally be the trigger for his dad to get in touch with him. Once Tom realized Martin's behaviour had nothing to do with him but was an expression of the boy's grief over his father's absence, he could be sympathetic and supportive instead of angry and hurt over what he had felt was a rejection of himself.

However, having difficulties with the Package Deal more often involves the problems stepparents have in accepting that their new partner isn't a singleton. When Billy moved in with Adele and her two children, 15-year-old Joe and 12-year-old Paul, he all but ignored them. Their father had left to live with Adele's best friend, so not only did she lose her husband and her best friend, she lost many of her friends and even relatives who got caught up in the bitter split. Adele felt unable to continue living in the town in which it had all happened, so she took her children to live several hundred miles away. Because of this they lost touch with school friends and relatives as well as leaving the home and the area they had grown up in. They had watched their mother struggle to make ends meet, looking after them and holding down a full-time job at the same time. When Billy came along, Joe and Paul were thrilled. They could see how much he meant to their mother and how happy she was with him. They were delighted at the thought that she would be able to share part of the responsibility for earning a living and keeping a house with him – they already did their bit around the house. They looked forward to having a man living with them – someone to play football with, to come and watch them play rugby who could understand the rules. They were friendly and welcoming – and it took some time for them to become thoroughly disenchanted.

Billy worked hard at keeping ties with his own children, 13-year-old Stephanie and 11-year-old Pete. He insisted on their coming to stay every weekend, even though this made them grumpy – it meant they often missed out on school sports and parties with their friends. There were four bedrooms, but Paul had to share with his brother when Stephanie and Pete came so that both of them could have their own rooms – Pete took over Paul's while

Faking it

This is probably the only time a counsellor or agony aunt will tell you faking it can be a good thing! Faking emotion usually means lying, and lying in any relationship is simply asking for trouble. The problem is that when a lie is found out – and they are usually found out – you then have to deal with fallout not only from the original difficulty, but from the anger and hurt of discovering you've been deceived. And lying usually means you're covering something up and thus never have the incentive to sort out whatever it is you're hiding. But in stepfamilies, there is a place for faking it.

Having affection or love, or even tolerance, for children who are not your own isn't easy. You grow up with your children; many parents don't fall instantly in love with their own kids, but many do, or at least they find that the bond grows in the first few hours, days or weeks after having them. It's gut-deep and you have very little choice about it. Even when you don't like what your kids do, you can't help loving them. Another person's child is a different thing. You don't have that bond, and you may even have primeval reasons for actively disliking, fearing or being wary of them. After all,

Stephanie had her own room. Billy made little effort with his stepsons – he tolerated the children living with him rather than trying to make a relationship with them. He wouldn't play football with them or go and watch them when they played sports for their school. He never took them out for a meal, although he insisted on taking his kids out for burgers or pizza at least once a weekend. And his attitude rubbed off on his kids – Stephanie and Pete were offhand with Joe and Paul, they made no effort to be friendly or cooperative and ignored polite requests to respect the boys' belongings when they were in the house. Things came to a head when Paul came back from playing rugby

their existence proves that the person you love was loved by, and loved, someone before you. The children will have their own reasons for finding you an intruder or an affront, and it can all lead to hostility at worst, indifference at best. Some stepparents say they'll be nice to the child when the child begins to be nice to them. It doesn't work that way – you're the adult so it should begin with you. And however you actually feel about them, this is the time to be really big and grown-up, and at least ACT nice. There's an interesting experiment you can try. Think about the way horror films make you scared, or romantic films make you feel soppy, by showing you people, often staring straight into the camera and thus straight at you, showing these emotions. Stand in front of a mirror and make a really scared face. As you look at yourself, you'll start feeling panicky. Then look warm and kind and loving; you'll begin to feel the same. Fake it with the kids. Be relentlessly nice, kind, understanding, accepting … even though it is killing you to do so in the face of anger, rejection or unresponsiveness. Keep it up. Sooner or later two things will happen. One is that they'll begin to accept it, and to respond in kind. The second is that you'll begin to feel it for real. Takes time, takes effort. But it really is worth it.

one Saturday afternoon: while he had been out Pete had spent the entire time in the bedroom Pete considered his own, and while there had broken Paul's new PlayStation and eaten a whole unopened box of chocolates his grandmother had given him for his birthday. When Paul complained, Billy said it was his own fault for leaving them in 'Pete's' bedroom. The resulting row ended with Billy hitting Paul, and Adele decided enough was enough. If Billy wasn't prepared to be a stepfather to her children as well as a father to his own, she didn't want the relationship to continue.

Billy's behaviour was an extreme version of ignoring the Package Deal, but many stepparents fall into the same trap without realizing it. There can be no doubt that it's difficult to love your stepchildren in the same way as you might your own. A new family means everyone is catapulted immediately into having to deal with a **multiple extended family** and all that goes with it. The fact that you don't feel as strong a love for them as you do their parent, your new partner, can have you feeling there is something wrong. Maybe, you think, it's the child's fault – they aren't lovable, they are bad and hostile. Or maybe it's your own fault – there is something missing in you because you can't summon up feeling for them. What often happens then is that the adult withdraws and gives up. If you can't feel love straight away, you believe, it stands to reason you never will. So you may concentrate on the love you feel for and the relationship you have with the adult, or with your own children – or, indeed, for one particular child for whom you do feel some emotion or bond. When Chris moved in with Tracie, he and her children got on quite well. Then things started going wrong. They hit one dramatic and significant problem, but at the root of some of their difficulties was the fact that he found it hard to make the effort. He had had an instant feeling of very strong love for his own sons when they were born, and got on well with Abigail, but he found most of her children more challenging. And finding them hard work, he soon gave up. He simply hadn't realized that he might have to make efforts at this – that along with Tracie and his own came the already formed family into which he had to fit and find a place. Ade too found fault with Daniel while adoring his own twin sons. He couldn't summon up loving feelings for him, and felt that he ought to.

The fact that the arriving adult has to **find their place** is perhaps one of the basic complications in stepfamilies. As adults we are used to the idea that children fit around us – that we set the rules, the agenda, the boundaries. After all, in first-time families the whole point is that you make your relationship with your partner and then children arrive; you're there first. So to a certain extent the idea that you come first and the kids fit in around you is how it should be, as it usually is. It's not good for children to run households, to have their needs and wishes overriding all else. Children who have all their needs instantly satisfied grow up demanding, selfish and endlessly discontented. But it is necessary at least to know what their needs are and to accommodate them as much as is appropriate and realistic. Children who never have their needs satisfied at all grow up with little self-worth, convinced they are never going to have what they require. Neither extreme is good. For healthy development children require a mixture of satisfaction and having to learn they must wait or occasionally not get what they want. The balance is important, so it is vital to recognize that it's a whole different ball game when you have a separated family. Children may be more demanding and needy because of what has happened to them in the break-up of their family, or they may be less, having sadly learnt that they don't get what they want. When it comes to moving a new partner into an existing family, it is essential for the adults concerned to recognize that they are the new face on the block. The children were there first, and have every right and every reason to expect you to be aware of and make allowances around that.

A stepfamily can be a second chance for everyone concerned, in lots of different ways. Joe and Paul had hoped it would be a second chance to have a father-like figure who would do all the things they hoped and expected a dad would do – support and love their mum, play with them, show an interest in them and their pursuits. For Chris, it was an opportunity to have a family in addition to the babies he and Tracie had. Once they had got over the misunderstanding that had driven a wedge between them, he and his

Message board

Viewers of the Stepfamilies TV series will have seen me ask every family to put up a Message Board – I also sometimes called it a Boast Board. It's a way to make it clear that everyone in your family has a position and a role there – a place where you can post chore rotas and keep your calendar. It may be where you leave messages and reminders to each other. But it's also where you can pin all sorts of material to celebrate and pull your family together. Up there go photos, school certificates and drawings. You can invite any member of your family to stick up anything that they've seen they'd like to draw to the attention of other people – cartoons, magazine or newspaper cuttings, letters. It's a way of making a mark and of providing continuity. It's a way of keeping in touch. It says that everyone who contributes has a say, even if they're not there all the time or haven't been there very long. Sticking something on the message board says you have a place in the house, that it's your and their house, and home, too. Some families divide the board up into sections – one for each member. Others stick things all over, higgledy-piggledy. Others pin up an envelope for each person so others can put messages for that person in it. You can arrange your message board to suit your home and your family.

stepchildren began to build a relationship that he enjoyed and valued. For some adults, myself included, it is a chance to have a child when otherwise that opportunity might not have existed. I couldn't have my own, but I am not a mother-figure to my stepson since he had a perfectly good mother already – he describes me as a 'significant other'. I, on the other hand, feel I have a son in him. And a better son I couldn't have wished for. For fathers like Ali, the new family gives a chance of redemption – to be a better stepfather to his partner Sonia's two sons than he had been a father first time round to his son and daughter, and a chance to try again at being a good father to his own too. These opportunities – to get it right, to make it better, to have something you might otherwise not have had – are all available … if the stepparent accepts the Package Deal.

Of course, accepting the Package Deal can be less than helpful sometimes. Tim was delighted to have acquired a new family in linking up with Lynn. He loved Ryan and Rebecca so much and wanted so much to do right by them that he felt the best thing for him to do was to take over – to be the only dad in their lives. He was angry at their father for losing touch soon after he split from Lynn and felt he was a far better parent to the kids than Steve was or could be. He was hurt and upset that, as he saw it, Ryan didn't appreciate him. Tim made it very clear he hated either of them seeing their dad. He'd never ban them or stop them seeing Steve, but talked in front of them about how much it hurt him. Rebecca, who loved Tim, responded by feeling she had to choose sides. In her eyes, she couldn't have both of them so she plumped for the one she lived with – Tim. This caused enormous pain and confusion to Ryan and Steve, and would have had distressing consequences for Rebecca herself if she had maintained this stand. Fortunately, Tim and Steve had the enormous courage and maturity to overcome their hostility and to agree to work together – to be the two dads, Dad and Stepdad, to their two shared children.

But sadly many parents and stepparents refuse to cooperate in this way. And many stepparents find it well nigh impossible to cope with the mixed feelings they have towards the children of another person and to accept them in their own homes or in the lives of their partners, with sad results. It's not uncommon, and it's very human, for someone to get jealous of or angry towards some aspects of a partner's previous life and ask them to forget or remove these elements. It's one thing to insist certain friends, pets, photographs or belongings be airbrushed out of the picture. It's quite another to require that children go too. When Cameron was 10 his father remarried, to a women who really took against her new husband's son. She was frosty when her husband was there, but actually violent when Cameron was left alone with her. It came to a showdown when Cameron's mother found out and refused to let her son be abused any longer. His father had to decide whether to bow to the fact that his new wife was unable to accept his son or insist she had to take Cameron on too. He chose the former, and it was ten years before his second marriage broke down and he tried to reunite with Cameron. Who by that time had written his father out of his life, and wanted nothing more to do with him. The reality is that when you have children, whether those children were chosen and planned or not, you take on a lifetime responsibility. And if you start a relationship with anyone who already has a family, that responsibility is part of the life you receive into your own. If you really aren't prepared to take on the Package Deal, you shouldn't be prepared to take them on. It's as simple as that.

Things to Keep in Mind

- With stepfamilies, it's a case of What You See Is What You Get. You can't pick and choose and ignore the fact that there are children there as well. Even if children live with their other parent, they will still be an important part of your life, and you of theirs.

- The other parent's influence will always be there to some degree, whether they are still a physical presence or not. Living in a stepfamily means you will have to accept the existence, needs and wishes of a child or stepchild's other parent.

- When there are children on both sides, you need to make a special, conscious effort to spread your attention and not just to concentrate on your own.

- If you are the incoming adult, remember that you are coming into an already established family. You're the grown up. It is you who will have to negotiate, compromise and adjust to what is already there and to the differences there might be in your lifestyles.

- All our natural instincts fight against making another person's child 100 per cent your own. Don't frustrate yourself by trying for or demanding what may be an unattainable ideal. It's a time to be a 'good enough parent' again.

- If you really can't accept the Package Deal, you shouldn't be there. Tough, but true.

Chapter 6

Coming Late to the Scene

In the traditional, first-time, family one of you may be older than the other, but even so you will be at the same stage in life: beginners in the family stakes. In a stepfamily, whether you are similar ages or from a different generation, the one significant difference between your relationship and that of a first-time one is that you may both be coming to it at very different times in your lives. Partners may be out of step with each other in the experiences and expectations they have of family life. For instance, one may be in their twenties, with no experience of children, the other in late thirties or forties and a parent of teenagers. For 28-year-old Ben it was particularly hard to find his place in Tina's family. She had two sons, of 24 and 14, and two daughters, of 19 and 12. With only a few years between them, her children refused to see him as a father-figure. Ben felt he simply hadn't learnt the skills to deal with teenagers – something that most parents have at least thirteen years to practise! However, since he was now their mother's partner, Ben felt he should be seen as equal to her and that the best way to deal with it was to try to be adult and parental. This led to furious rows with the 24-year-old who, quite reasonably, didn't see why he should be lectured to and told how to behave by someone no older than some of his own friends.

Adults **coming into an established family** may feel ill at ease, wondering how they should behave and whether they should try to be parents or friends. The children concerned may see any new adults as interlopers invading their territory and react accordingly. Perhaps the most important and significant aspect of coming late to the scene is that you or your partner may be playing catch-up all the time. Even babies have their own strong personalities, but at least when they are yours you're there from the beginning. Parent and child have the time to learn about each other as the offspring grow up and you grow into being their parent. They do have aspects and characteristics which will be theirs and theirs alone, but equally there will be plenty they pick up from you – tastes and jokes and shared experiences. When you come into a family, even when the children are quite young, you come into something that has got going without you. It's like joining a group halfway through the evening and finding you don't understand half the punchlines and have no idea what they might be referring to in most of the anecdotes or discussions. The children will have qualities and interests and have had experiences you in no way share. Even parents are fond of saying, as they survey the results of a quarrel, 'S/he didn't get that from me!' When it's a stepchild you are talking about, this is entirely true. They may have a sense of humour you can't understand, many enjoy pastimes that are a complete mystery to you or even directly opposed to anything you like or find acceptable. When Chris joined Tracie and her five children, he frequently clashed with her daughter Kat. Neither could make head nor tail of the other's sense of humour. Both used irony and sarcasm, but it was as if they spoke another language – they'd each end up thinking the other was out to hurt.

It's actually one of the griefs of being a parent that as they develop you begin to understand that your children are separate beings with tastes and ideas of their own. But at least you have the foundation of years of love and trust on which to build a new relationship. You know they need you and appreciate you, in spite of tears and tantrums as they grow up and away from you. But a stepparent may have no such foundation. When you find yourself clashing with and unable to understand your new family members, you may decide it's their fault or yours and there's no point in trying. In addition, those glimpses of a personality unlike yours may feel painful. It underlines that the family and your new partner had a life before you, and that someone else was there instead. The personality clash may be one that any two people can have – even parents can find themselves having differences with their own child. But it could be that the similarity with the other parent is what makes it hard for a new partner.

A newcomer to a family may be acutely aware of the relationship between their partner and the partner's ex, and their new stepchildren and both their parents. They may find the way all of them get on hard to cope with. Of course, in many families there is enormous hostility between the exes, but in most cases the children concerned are trying to keep the link. This constant glimpse of otherness, of difference, only serves to highlight the fact that everything in this family began long before you or your new partner joined it – and that can be painful.

This may be the first shot at parenthood for you or your partner. You need to remember that whatever their circumstances, for the kids this is at least the second time around in having a parent. Which means that when looking at a new adult, they will have comparisons to make. What sort of a mum or dad do you make in contrast to their own? Children may delight in catching you out in being a novice at being a parent at all or being a novice with them.

There may be all sorts of feelings of rivalry, resentment and bitterness washing around too. Sometimes children have had a period of living with a parent on their own – either after a death or separation or while a family is breaking up – and one parent may be physically or emotionally absent. They may have got used to managing on their own – them and one parent against the world. They may spend far more time with a single parent than they might if that adult had to share their free time among children and partner. And all the children, or one particular one, may have taken on a special status caring for or being leant on by the parent. When a new partner comes along, they may make comparisons with the missing parent, who they will feel loyalty towards whatever their behaviour during and after the split. But they may also set themselves up for comparison too. There may be rivalry – particularly intense between older children who have taken on the status of being the man or woman of the house, or at least their missing parent's representative there.

Young people may take out their resentment at the break-up of their family on the nearest and likeliest target – the newcomer. This newcomer may not be the cause of the break-up or even the reason their parents don't get back together again. Being late on the scene, however, means that you may be the one they feel would be least missed and thus best blamed. All the bitterness may be dumped on the latest addition to the family as they take out their feelings of loss and pain on you.

However much you love your new partner, creating a stepfamily is going to put a **strain on your relationship**. You may be crossing time lines in linking up with them. You may be going back to being a parent of young children at a time in your life when you thought you'd left the nappy or toddler stage behind you. Or you may be leaping ahead to having teenagers without the slow lead up through having babies, toddlers and children. It's not only a possible lack of experience, or resentment at having to do it all again, that causes stress. It's a dislocation in what feels natural and correct.

We tend to assume that life will follow a fairly orderly and logical pattern. You expect to go from being a baby yourself through the various stages of growing up – baby, toddler, child, teenager and young adult. As a young adult, you expect to experiment with love and relationships and eventually to find someone with whom you settle down. Courtship is followed by nest-building as the two of you, together, create a home for yourselves. In time, there's a pregnancy and a baby. Maybe two or three or more. You guide them through babyhood, toddlerhood, childhood, the teenage years and young adulthood. You go from being a young couple to parents, to being middle-aged, to having an empty nest, to being retired and eventually old. At each stage there are the feelings, the behaviour, the patterns that feel appropriate and right.

But a stepfamily can throw all that up into the air. Someone such as Ali can go back to having young children around, having already gone through the nappies and primary school stage ten years previously. Tim inherited a family with a 5- and a 9-year-old and went from being a childfree bachelor to acting as a father of two in one jump. He had had a short experience of a baby when his own son was born nine years previously, but lost contact soon after. And Ian joined his partner Denise and her three, 15-year-old Amy, 12-year-old Vikki and 11-year-old Sam, with no previous experience of having children at all. The temptation, as an adult, when you feel out of your depth is to bluff. Ben tried to deal with his acute discomfort and feelings of insecurity and lack of confidence by acting as he thought a father would – by lecturing and hectoring, laying down the law and appearing as if he knew it all. He and his 24-year-old stepson had stand-up rows that caused major offence and upset. Ben felt that as their stepfather he had the right, if not the obligation, to give advice. Not only did the 24-year-old fail to see why he should listen to someone who had only been in the family a few months, he really objected to being told what to do by someone who did not have the advantage of experience and the wisdom of age but had been at school with him.

Second families can bring together not only adults at **different life stages**, but children too. Sofia's children were teenagers at school while their stepsiblings were at very different phase in their lives – getting married and finishing university. As it happened, both sides found it rather fun to suddenly acquire much younger/older stepsiblings. But not all families do appreciate

Chore Chart

Creating a chore chart was another strategy I used in the TV series *Stepfamilies*, to bring a family together. Sharing chores can be a way of positioning newcomers, whether adults or kids, in a new family. Children need to do chores, even if one of the adults living in your house is a stay-at-home full-time parent. Why? It's important for everyone in a stepfamily to show respect to each other and to be seen as being treated equally. Doing chores is a leveller. It also gives a sense of ownership and responsibility. This is your home, and doing something to keep it running smoothly shows it. Even very young children, and children who only live there part-time, should have their chores, as a way of claiming their place and being involved. And adults should share the work equally too, even if they go out to work all day.

How should you draw up a chore chart? For it to be something that everyone 'buys into' and agrees, it's best to make it a cooperative effort. But it does help for one person in the family to take responsibility for managing it and making it run.

First, everyone agree what chores need doing. Different families have different ideas of what's important, so come to your own agreement. You might also want to agree on what might be 'extra' chores, such as this difference. Seventeen-year-old Eamon deeply resented the arrival in his life of stepsiblings 3-year-old Gabriel and 4-year-old Haley. Eamon's parents had separated when he was 12 and he stayed with his father every weekend and one night a week. When Gabriel and Haley and their mother moved in, Eamon lost his own room and the private time he spent with his father. The children were boisterous, energetic, curious and adventurous, and Eamon complained that he couldn't leave any belongings at the house or they'd be interfered with. The home he had had with his father changed from a serene, adult

washing cars or mowing lawns, and negotiate whether these can be done as paid-for chores. Some families may want to tie chores into pocket money – you get it if you complete your chores, or the amount you get is dependent on chores. My personal view is that this introduces an element of 'Shall I, shan't I?' into the equation. I don't think you'd be very amused if Mum or Dad felt it was optional and depended on how they felt that day as to whether you get your evening meal or not. In the same light, I think whether or not you do your chores should be approached as similarly non-negotiable. Everyone does chores. No argument.

Draw up a list of chores, and assign them on a rolling schedule to everyone. You might like to give everyone a mixture of easy, medium and hard chores each period. Or you might opt for each person having easy, medium or hard weeks. Whatever, the idea is that each week chores rotate so that everyone gets a go at all of them, with some allowance for age, height and weight. On the whole, share out chores equally – that's the essence of being in a family; everyone pulls their weight and does their part.

Agree what you're going to do, and then draw up a written agreement or contract setting it out. Ask everyone to sign the contract – 'We, the undersigned, agree …' Review the contract regularly, and if it's not working, go back to the table to discuss why not and what you'd like to do to make it work.

retreat to a noisy, family-centred one. Eamon said he might have been able to get on with stepsiblings near his own age – these two simply infuriated and embarrassed him. The only time he accompanied his father and the two children to town they bumped into some of his friends. Eamon was mortified at the idea of his friends knowing that his father was now living with a younger woman. Most teenagers cringe at the idea of their own parents being sexual, or displaying sexual behaviour to their friends – Eamon felt a young family showed up his father, and him. And things came to a head when his father told him a new baby was on the way. By the time his stepmother gave birth, Eamon no longer stayed over with his father. They spoke on the phone, they would meet for a burger or pizza, but Eamon wouldn't go to the house.

However, many stepfamilies can make an advantage of that mismatch in ages. Young people who might resent the loss of a parent's sole attention could come round if they feel having a small child around gives them some status – and some love. Thirteen-year-old Sian lived with her father and younger brother before Sharon joined them with her two younger children. Sian is now the eldest of four rather than two, and at times is the trusted carer of a 3-year-old; a responsibility that she rises to and values. Small children may pick up on atmospheres, becoming grizzly and fretful when surrounded by tension or anger. But they seldom understand why the negative emotions are there, or choose sides. So while older children may be hostile to a newcomer, a small child may be welcoming and loving and bridge the gap between the two families.

Tony adored 4-year-old Jem because, having only been 2 when he arrived, she loved him wholeheartedly and accepted him as a father, unlike his new partner Talia's other children. This did in itself lead to one further problem, as Tony and Talia allowed Jem to apparently believe Tony was her natural father, thinking she didn't remember a time before and without him. Trying to fudge the fact that the stepparent is coming late to the scene when one or more children are assumed to be too young to remember is tempting, but dangerous. It may drive a wedge between siblings, some of whom know only too well that the newcomer is a step not a full parent, and others who seem in blissful ignorance, and store up problems for later. Tony and Talia realized Jem needed to know the truth that Tony was certainly her father in his love and care for her, but wasn't her birth father, but kept putting off the moment to tell her.

Coming late to the scene can also make **relationships between siblings** difficult even when they are not hostile – in fact, especially when they become more than friendly. Stepsiblings have no legal relationship with each other, even when their parents marry. Coming from different homes and upbringings, they may meet and far from being in conflict, may fall for each other. Living together especially can give them the time and the proximity to become emotionally close. This can cause immense problems. Their parents, friends and family may still consider them to be siblings, even if the law says they have no tie, and be shocked or against such a friendship. And the new Sexual Offences Act does include stepsiblings under its definition of 'family' when setting out what may be considered to be abusive sex, even when consent is given. Under this definition, if stepsiblings have a relationship and one of them is under 18, one or even both of them could be considered to have broken the law.

Of course, there can be tremendous advantages to children with a stepparent and indeed stepsiblings coming late to the scene. One problem with parents and their own children is that they get used to each other. As a parent, you can remember when little Johnny wanted above all to be a train driver and you may not have caught up to the fact that his new interest is quantum physics. A new stepparent comes with a fresh eye and no preconceptions, and may give children more respect and a better listening ear than their own parent. One trick to keep in mind is that you don't want, under any circumstances and in any shape of family, to try to replace the missing parent. You aren't a mum or dad to them and never will be. You are a stepmum or stepdad – but don't see that as second best. Being a Significant Other and doing the job well is infinitely better than trying to be a second-hand parent and failing. With an age gap you may find yourself falling naturally into being a sort of big sibling – as I did – or a grandparent; someone who is close but objective. And that is so often what children need to have, as well as having parents. However, what they don't want in you is a friend, even if you are close in age. What kids need from parent-figures is parental care – you should be friendly, but also maintain a certain authority. What Ben got wrong was not the recognition that he should be something other than a fellow bloke in his twenties, but the degree and the manner in which he assumed parental authority. If he'd stepped sideways and acted as a big brother to his partner's children, as I acted as a big sister to my stepson, he might have been more accepted by them.

The advantage to your children in suddenly having stepsiblings sprung upon them is that it often fills in gaps. A child who has always longed for a brother or sister may get their wish. They could have had it if you'd had another child – but not an older or similar-aged sibling, which a new family can deliver. When Zach married Mina his son Ethan and daughter Kim started visiting regularly, joining Mina's daughter Amber. Amber had always wanted a twin sister – and not only was Kim her own age and in the same class at school but the two of them shared many interests. They had been friends before their parents got together; now the two of them slipped with great delight into being sisters.

However, same-age stepsiblings aren't the only ones to welcome a new family. When a generation gap means new stepsiblings are much older or younger it can help in that there may be no rivalry between kids who occupy such different worlds and needs – some at secondary school or college, others at nursery or primary. When Ali's son and daughter finally settled back into a relationship with him, both of them enjoyed his new partner Sonia's children, who were ten or so years younger than them.

Having a new baby between the new partners can also throw up all sorts of issues. On the one hand, it may create a bond and a bridge between children from both sides. In having a Mine, Yours and Ours, you give mine and yours a blood link to each other and to both parents. They may not be related to the steps, but they are to the new baby and through them to the other members of this group. Playing with and showing off the baby to their friends and relatives gives them the opportunity to explore how they feel about the new arrangement – to talk about it with others and come to terms with it. It can help them feel competent and in control, as they gain the skills to care for a child. But it can also trigger hurt, fears of rejection and rage. They may feel redundant – not only have you hived off their other parent, now you're moving in a child to take their place. And like Eamon, they may simply be embarrassed at your making it so obvious you still Do Sex, at this late stage in your and their lives.

If the adults and children at the centre of a family can find coming late to the scene hard, how do some grandparents find it? In the traditional order of things, grandparents see their grandchildren born and growing up. Some grandparents may have less contact than others and find it hard to know or keep up with their grandchildren, but underlying it all is the knowledge that they were there from the beginning, and they are family. With a stepfamily, grandparents stand on the sidelines as one family comes apart and perhaps one set of grandchildren moves away and loses touch. And all of a sudden, they can be presented with another child or group of kids and told, 'These are your grandchildren now.' We'll deal in detail with these issues in a later chapter, but for now it's worth considering that everything I might have said about new stepparents struggling to keep up with new children whose characteristics, personality and tastes they may not understand or share, may go double for grandparents. And it can be particularly confusing if a relationship with one partner significantly older than the other puts new stepgrandparents uncomfortably near or very far in age from the new in-law and children. Just the fact that these new family members feel so alien and unfamiliar, while holding a position that makes you feel you ought to be close to them, can trigger some people to feel anger, hostility or remoteness. New children and their parent may be felt to be a cuckoo in the nest – and be blamed for the break-up of the old family, the loss of contact with other grandchildren and all sorts of ills, even if it has nothing to do with them.

Things to Keep in Mind

● The newcomer to a stepfamily has joined a group that will have started without them. They will have to play catch-up, so don't get frustrated if they don't 'get it' immediately.

● Don't be upset if at first the new stepparent feels like an outsider. In time, they will blend in and it will feel like their family too.

● It will be second-time-around parenting for any children in the stepfamily. Expect natural comparisons with their birth parent and don't be hurt.

● Being in a stepfamily scrambles up the usual time-scale. The first experience of having a 'baby', for example, could be a strapping teenager. Or one of you may jump back to having nappies or toddlers when they did that stage years ago. The children involved may also be struggling to bridge age differences, with, say, a set-in-their-ways teen suddenly having to cope with a hyperactive 3-year-old.

● Having a new baby of your own can be a boon or a bombshell to the existing children in a stepfamily. The more you involve them and discuss with them, the better.

● Don't take it personally. Any of it!

Chapter 7

Family Structures

We've touched on the issue of gaining a new set of sons, daughters, brothers or sisters in the last chapter, but we do need to consider this aspect of stepfamilies in some detail.

It's one thing to have one child; then maybe have another; then, after much thought and consultation with your partner, decide to have a third or even a fourth. That is not how it happens in stepfamilies! One day you're a mother or father of none or one or two or three. And the next, you've been instantly catapulted into a family of double or triple that size – and it's a shock to the system. Non-parents have to catch up with how to manage screaming toddlers or teenage tearaways. Parents of small children have to learn how to negotiate with strong-minded adolescents. Someone who thought they had left the tantrum or nappy stage long behind may find themselves back to square one. Above all, everyone has to adjust to what it means to have more people in the house than you have previously known.

It's not just a case of where everyone goes. Tracie and her children made way for Chris. When Tracie and Chris's two babies, Joshua and Thomas, came along they had to move from a three- to a four-bedroom house that is still too small for them all. All the children have to share a bedroom and the smallest baby, Thomas, sleeps in his parents' room. It's a tight fit and sometimes the noise level is high, and everyone craves some peace and quiet or some privacy. But far more important is the fact that you may find managing more children than you have grown accustomed to confusing.

Human beings tend to engage in alliances with those around them. Two parents and one child may fall into a pattern of the two adults being together with the child feeling a bit left out. Or one parent and the child creating their own little world with the other parent feeling neglected. Both patterns may be maintained, or you may glide from one to the other from day to day. When there are two children, they may form a group of their own, or each adult may gravitate towards a combination of one parent and a child together. With more children, they may gang up, two against one other or two against another two. In each family there are either firm alliances or a variety of shifting patterns of who supports and likes whom best.

When you **introduce a new family**, the whole thing can go ballistic. In Chris and Tracie's new family, Joanne had always felt the odd one out in relation to her three older siblings, because they had regular contact with their dad and she did not. With the arrival of Chris she felt even more isolated since he formed a strong bond with Joanne's younger sister, Abigail, and his two sons, Joshua and Thomas. From feeling left out, Joanne went to feeling totally abandoned and deprived. She and her older sister Kat frequently linked up and were good friends, but at times Joanne still felt the outsider. One of the bonuses of working on their stepfamily issues for Joanne was that it led to her birth father getting back in touch.

It can be very hard to keep track, as from day to day certain children may range from being total enemies to total friends with someone else in the new arrangement. This happens in first-time families too, don't forget. It's just that there is more potential and more opportunity for it to happen when the family suddenly becomes larger, with new people coming into an existing unit. And the battles can be that much more vicious when the newcomers are unrelated to you, as they are in a stepfamily. You may be angry with and feel you hate a sibling, but at the bottom they are family, and family will forgive you, love you and be there for you. When you blame a 'steppie' for getting in your face, for trespassing on your territory, for taking the attention and love of a parent, there is no such comfortable fall-back. You have no history with them and it can be hard to forgive or come to terms with what is happening. As an adult watching this all happen, you have to keep your wits about you to keep up with who is in, who is out, who are friends and who are enemies. Above all, you need to recognize that a new family structure will have an impact and plan accordingly.

It will also have an effect on you and your behaviour. Adults entering a new stepfamily may have had a period of being single parents. Even if the actual break-up of the previous family is quite fresh, you may still have been operating as a parent on your own. Your ex might have been living apart from you, or just been there in body but 'not there' in spirit. You and your children may have got used to working together as a unit, and may find it difficult to throw open the gates and let anyone else in. When Tracie and Chris found the going tough in their new family, Tracie suddenly realized that she still acted as if she was a single mum. When someone needed pulling up short, or the family needed a talking-to, Tracie did it on her own. Worse than that, she was in the habit of delivering a lecture to the whole family as if they were naughty toddlers ... and including Chris as one of the people told off. Partly, she felt his attitude at the time didn't help. But partly it was because she simply wasn't used to working as one of two adults in a partnership; she was used to being the single parent, responsible for it all. She had to make the effort – and she did, brilliantly – to stand side by side with Chris and work with him, not against him. She had, in effect, to give up and lose the role of chief mediator and peacekeeper in the family. This role gave her a lot of hard work so on one level she was delighted to lose it. But being the one in charge gives you status and importance in your own eyes as well as in other people's and that's why some find it hard to let go.

Adults establishing a new stepfamily may fondly think the children involved will not be greatly affected by acquiring **new stepsiblings**. But a child who suddenly goes from being the eldest, the middle one, the youngest, to having an older sibling or a rival for the place of youngest may be extremely upset. Not only do they lose a parent, they lose the certainty of who they are and what is their place and role in their family.

The place you hold in a family is very important and can affect your behaviour and even your character. Older children tend to be the ones who at best look after and at worst boss everyone else. They often feel responsible or put upon, and can grow up to be compulsive carers or the peacemakers or organizers of their family. Younger siblings can constantly feel they are trying to catch up with people bigger and better than them, and be competitive and defensive. Middle children often get left out and forgotten, and can beaver away in silence, suddenly surprising everyone with what's been on their mind for ages. Only children can find it easier to get on with adults than other kids, and have little experience of having to fight for attention at home. What happens when a stepfamily is formed is that the place a child may hold, and be secure in, suddenly changes. An only child is an only no longer. An oldest child can gain an older brother or sister and become a younger one. A middle child can find they have someone else to share their lonely, quiet, forgotten slot. A youngest child, the baby of the family, may suddenly find they have become the middle one with a younger new sibling – or even become the oldest in a new formation. The larger the new family, the more children can break up into mini-groups. In Tracie's and Chris's family, the eldest three formed a group, especially since they shared a father. But the youngest of that group, Kat, often allied with the next child, Joanna. And little Abigail, the next in line, went from being the youngest of the family to being a somewhat out-of-the-way middle child when Chris and Tracie had Joshua and Thomas and she became the oldest in that group of three.

A new structure can, however, be a plus for all concerned. When Russ married Sally, he brought three children to live four days a week with her and her three. She had two sons and a daughter, he had two daughters and a son. Sally and Russ were worried that having so many children in the house would lead to arguments. To their surprise, the new family got on surprisingly well. Her children had been an oldest son of 9, a middle daughter of 7 and a younger son of 5. His children had been an eldest daughter of 13, a middle daughter of 10 and a youngest son of 6. All of a sudden the 13-year-old girl became the oldest of six rather than three, and the 9-year-old boy went from eldest to middle. She loved the extra authority, he was delighted to no longer be expected to be grown-up and in charge of his siblings. Russ's second daughter, at 10, gained some status and felt very mature in being older than four children instead of having one above and one below. Sally's 7-year-old daughter also lost her middle position and was able to be the older sister of a 6-year-old brother as well as a 5-year-old sister. Russ's son jumped from being the baby of the family to having a younger sister, and she gained a slightly older brother whom she soon adored. The change in status and position and the novelty of, in effect, being new people actually smoothed over and helped the shift from small family to large one. Each of them found more advantages to the new position they held than disadvantages.

Of course, it doesn't always work that way. When Sharon and Andy joined their families of his daughter, 13-year-old Sian, and 9-year-old son Josh to her son, 11-year-old Josh, and daughter 3-year-old Rhiannon, Andy's Josh particularly found the adjustment hard. He adored his new baby sister and thoroughly enjoyed playing with her and looking after her. But he also mourned the loss of being the baby himself in his own family. Teenager Sian and 11-year-old Josh formed a new alliance, since they were close in age and both at secondary school. But this meant that younger Josh lost out on the closeness he used to share with his sister as she now spent most of her time with her newer younger brother. Indeed, since 9-year-old Josh lost his own bedroom to 11-year-old Josh and 3-year-old Rhiannon and had to share his sister Sian's room, he also took the brunt of her understandable annoyance and frustration at the new regime.

Even if they never see a stepsibling, their very existence has an effect on a new family. Ryan and Rebecca, for instance, knew their new stepfather Tim had a child from an early relationship. They could hardly avoid knowing, in spite of the fact that Tim never had any contact with him, since Tim's son was in the same school class as Ryan. Tim's son seemed to play absolutely no part in their lives at all. Except that his presence underlined the fact that Tim was being more than a little hypocritical in criticizing their father, Steve, for not being a good father in losing touch, when Tim himself had no contact at all. Whether they realized it or not, it also caused them some anxiety. Ryan angrily wanted no part of trusting Tim and leaning on him. Rebecca was almost frantic in her desire to secure Tim as her dad. In both cases, the fact that they knew about Tim's birth son suggested that their underlying fear might be that if they grew to rely on Tim, what was to stop him withdrawing from them as he had with his own son?

A new family may also throw up mixed feelings about the relative status of children and the new adult. Children who have taken on a supportive role after

All Move

A new family may mean a brand new home as you get together and move to somewhere you can all start afresh in. More often, it means one family moves in with another, or comes to stay with them.

Human beings are as territorial as any other animal. Children can feel understandably hostile at the idea of someone moving in on their room. It's not just the smaller space they now have – it's that they're having to make way for a stranger, and one they may have mixed feelings about anyway. It may seem practical to simply ask one child to welcome another into their bedroom, but it's worth considering the emotional cost of this.

Instead of simply shoehorning a new child into the present arrangement, it may be worth while throwing everything up in the air and starting again.

Look at all your available space, and allocate rooms so that everyone starts off in an unfamiliar place so you're all in the same position.

This may mean parents giving up the master bedroom if that would give children who have to share a fairer space.

Redecorating, with a colour scheme that everyone has agreed, helps too. It lets newcomers feel this is their home and the resident family feel it's a new beginning.

a break-up may feel in competition with a new adult, who not only seems to be usurping the missing parent's role but their own. When Vijay married Steph, he and her son Mark clashed head on. Steph, Mark and his sister Vikki had lived on their own for four years after the death of their father. At the funeral Mark's grandmother had told him, 'You'll have to be the man of the family now,' and the 11-year-old had taken her at her word. He'd been responsible and caring well beyond his years and taken on a supportive role to his mum. Now 15, he resented a new man coming into the family and not only trying to take the place of his father but trying to, as he saw it, oust him too. Steph and Mark thought he'd welcome the chance to go back to being a carefree teenager; he didn't. They fought over who should sit at the head of the table, who should have the armchair in the living-room, who should have first go with the TV remote. It was as if Mark felt that to let Vijay take away his position in the family would also finally mean the end of his father's continuing presence, in him. The fighting only stopped when Mark and Vijay sat down with a counsellor and worked out what was going on and why. Vijay was able to acknowledge and understand Mark's feelings and Mark was able to accept Vijay was doing his best and had no desire to do him down. They came to a compromise that involved several changes for all of them. Mark needed to see that his father would always be remembered and honoured, and Vijay and Steph learnt to talk about him freely to the children. Vijay and Steph needed to see Mark should have some responsibility in the home and not return to being an 11-year-old with nothing to do. Mark was formally given responsibility for certain chores and tasks, including being the one to choose where they all went on the summer holiday. When Vijay could accept that he wasn't there to replace but to supplement their late father, he and the children got on fine.

The shape and structure of the **old family may continue to haunt a new one** for some time. A parent may struggle to continue loving a child who reminds them strongly of an ex, especially after a bitter break-up or after a mourned death. Abiba found she had times of hating and feeling angry to the point of speechless rage with her daughter Nasha. She adored Nasha and loved being with her, but sometimes – and at first she couldn't understand why – she'd find herself gritting her teeth and flying off the handle at the child over very little. She finally realized it was because Nasha was the image of her father, whom Abiba had left after several years of a painful and destructive relationship. Nasha looked like him, spoke like him and acted like him. She also adored her father, so she often talked about him. Abiba would find herself tensing up and getting upset every time Nasha did something to bring him back into the house, if only in spirit. When Abiba realized what was happening and came to terms with the fact that her daughter had a right to consider her father fondly, she stopped taking out her resentment over the break-up on her beloved daughter.

Children losing a parent may try, consciously or unconsciously, to keep their presence alive by aping them. Saul was horrified to find his new children Alison and Ian were aggressive and abusive to their mother Gaby, and soon to him. Saul blamed their father Adrian, whom Gaby had divorced because of his violence. He felt Adrian had taught the kids how to behave. But it wasn't only Adrian who had an effect on their behaviour. The problem was that neither Saul nor Gaby had a good word to say about him, so all that the children heard about him was negative. Children love and miss their parents whatever, so the only way Alison and Ian could keep him 'with' them was to 'be' him, and the only things they knew of their father was his aggression and abusiveness. The situation changed when Gaby and Saul made a real effort to acknowledge the children's justified feelings, and to recall and talk about the good aspects of their father. All of a sudden they had better things to copy, and did.

Hats

One of the exercises we did in the TV series was aimed at helping family members understand their new family structure and adjust to it. We often assign roles to people, as you might plonk a hat on them. Josh and Ryan, for instance, were seen as the devils, the bad boys, of their families; the ones causing all the problems. Mums Lynn, Denise and Tracie were landed with being the peacemakers of their families, always having to mediate and settle quarrels. They were also the drudges, the ones accepted as having to do all the chores. We all have such roles in our family, or at school or work. 'Sheila? Oh, she's always been the joker in our family,' or 'You're just like your Uncle Fred, he was a rebel too.' Sometimes the labels seem complimentary: 'Who's Mummy's little helper?' or 'He's such a good child, never gives me any bother.' Sometimes they are more damaging: 'Your father was a no-good and you'll end up like just him.'

Imagine the roles in a family being like a set of fancy-dress hats, as for a party. It's as if these have to go round, and everybody must be dressed in one. Sometimes you pick your own costume. Mostly, you get what everyone else in the family or those around you hand you. The problem with these hats is that once you've got one you tend to be stuck with it. You might grow into the role – being seen as the Black Sheep means you might as well be bad, since nobody sees you in any other way. And even if you would like to change, it's hard, as none of your family will see you in any other way; you can behave perfectly and they'll still assume you're the Bad One. It's difficult enough when it's a bad hat – being seen as the problem and the troublemaker is distressing. But even a nice hat can be a burden. Always having to live up to being the Little Angel or the Princess is no joke. You may begin to feel you want to break out and refuse to always be Mother's Little Helper, but can't. The result may be years of being good ending in a sudden rebellion.

Look at these words. Can you find descriptions that fit you and your own family? Can you add any more hats?

Mother's Little Helper	Wee Willy Winky the Sleepyhead
Bad Child	Dreamer
Mr Fixit	Sulker
The King or Queen	Little Princess
The Monster	The Angel
The Joker	The Little Madam
Peacemaker	Hard Worker
The Quiet One behind a Veil	Black Sheep
Chief Cook	The Winner
The Household Maid	

You could write these down on slips of paper or even assemble paper or dressing-up hats to represent them. Get together with your own family and see who lands which role, by common agreement. Are you comfortable in these roles? Who says you suit your label? Do they really fit? Would you or they prefer not to wear their role? You don't have to stay with the one you've been handed. You can throw it off and be something more flexible, something more comfortable. But you can only do that if you look at and consider what role you've been landed with and why.

A new adult may find it hard to come to terms with the constant reminder, in the presence of a child, that someone else was there first. Liz, for instance, came into a house in which the eldest daughter, Hannah, had had several years of being the mother of the house after her own mum died. Liz took a great pride in being as perfect a mother as possible, cooking, washing, ironing and cleaning to give everyone the perfect home. She took over, 'retired' Hannah from doing any of it, and then felt she wasn't appreciated. She missed the fact that Hannah, far from feeling cared for, actually felt sidelined. Relations between Liz and Hannah were particularly frosty, and it wasn't until Liz realized that most of the hostility was on her part that things began to improve. The main problem was that Hannah was the image of her mother, whose photographs were dotted around the house. Every time Liz looked at Hannah, she felt her nose was rubbed in the fact that her husband had loved someone before her – and it was as if that person was still living with them. Liz had to learn to let go of her jealousy, to allow Hannah some responsibility back, to stop trying to be the perfect mother and just be 'good enough'. Hannah had to make some adjustment too. She had to see that loving and keeping alive the memory of her own mum didn't have to mean she should be enemies with her successor. It's often hard for children to recognize you can like a stepparent and not have that take anything away from the parent. As Rebecca eventually realized, you can have two fathers – a Dad at home and a Daddy you regularly visit. In families where children divide their time between homes, they may find themselves either deciding for themselves or responding to pressure to choose sides. Will used to take stepson Ethan with him and his own sons to football, until Ethan suddenly announced he didn't want to go. Sadly, Ethan had caught on to his own father's anxiety at losing his son's love to a rival, and realized he had to keep a distance to keep his dad happy.

In many stepfamilies, the loss of a parent may also mean the apparent **loss of a sibling**, too. In Sharon and Andy's new family, her son Josh and his daughter Sian, and his son Josh and her daughter Rhiannon, formed new alliances. Which would have been very comforting and would have helped to bring the family as a whole together, if it had not been for the fact that hand in hand with this came hostility on her Josh's part to his Josh. Going with her stepbrother, Sian followed the lead of most of the family in targeting her own brother as 'the problem'. Among many other losses occasioned by the split of his original family and the formation of this new one, the younger Josh thus also lost the good relationship he used to have with his sister. And he hardly gained a new one, as Sharon was intensely protective of her daughter and made strenuous efforts to keep 9-year-old Josh away from her, fearing he would harm her.

Ryan also felt he had lost his own sister, Rebecca. She sided with Tim and wanted nothing more to do with her own father, while Ryan wanted to keep in contact. Ryan felt Tim came between him and Rebecca, and resented what he saw as Tim flaunting his loving relationship with his stepdaughter, almost as an attack on Ryan.

It's very common for couples getting together in a new stepfamily, who might have brought Yours and Mine, to very quickly have an Ours. Sometimes, what might have been an exploratory relationship that may or may not have developed into a long-term, permanent one is catapulted into marriage or commitment by the arrival of **a shared baby**. Sometimes, one or other or both decide they really want a new child. This could either be to cement this relationship, or because they feel having a shared child will prove their love for each other. Sometimes it is because one of them either doesn't have children from a previous relationship, or has little contact with them and feels being a stepparent isn't enough – they want to be a parent to their own.

Many couples feel a family isn't real, isn't truly committed, unless there are children to hold you together. Whatever the rights or wrongs of that, the fact is that it often makes for large families, if you already have two, three, four or even five and your partner has several and then you bring another one or two into the equation – especially if your exes are meantime doing the same. That's an awful lot of half- and stepsiblings to keep track of! And don't forget that you may feel your ex's new children or stepchildren have nothing to do with you. They will, however, impinge on your children, who visit and keep in contact with their other parent and so have to come to terms with living with step- and half-siblings in those homes, as they may also be trying to do in your own house.

Sometimes a new baby is divisive. Existing children can feel cast off and pushed out. Ade found it easy to lavish love and attention on his twin sons, while his stepson Daniel looked on. He found it much harder to give Daniel the same level of affection and attention. Whether they live with the baby or see him or her on visits, the feeling may be: 'I'm not good enough – now they've got a new one they won't want me.' But often the baby provides a bridge between new adults and children. After all, children may feel they have absolutely no link to the new stepparent. Their own mother or father may love this new adult, but what is that to them? A baby, however, is a bond, sharing as it does a blood tie with the new adult and themselves. Babies are also fun and are talking points. In playing with, taking care of and talking to the baby, children can have something to share with a new adult with whom they might otherwise feel they have nothing in common. Above all, a new baby shifts the shape of the family and it may help children see themselves in a new light, no longer the youngest, or the eldest of two, or an only child or the piggy-in-the-middle, but a whole new person with a whole new family. It can shift the dynamics of the relationship with the new adult, moving it from suspicion, hostility or insecurity, to acceptance.

Of course, in some families different siblings may have different feelings and reactions to a newcomer, and this can drive a wedge between them as well as between themselves and a parent. When Noah married Mia he joined a household consisting of her and her two children, Keri and Jason. Jason had been 1 and Keri 6 when Noah arrived, and from the time he could talk Jason had always called Noah 'Dad'. The fact that Noah was neither of the older two children's birth father had become a family secret, never mentioned. Keri remembered a time before him but Jason did not – or not consciously, at least. When Keri was 10 and Jason 5, a new baby came along. Jason started teasing Keri, saying that she was different to him and the baby since Noah wasn't her father. Keri bit her lip at first, but she resented the baby enormously. Not only did Keri feel the new girl had taken her place in her mother's affections, she felt it had cut her off from her brother, and she was slow to forgive. Keri would have been superhuman to not have finally reacted as she did, and told Jason in no uncertain terms that on the contrary, she and he had more in common than he and the new child, since Noah was no father of his either. It was some time before Keri could forgive Noah or Mia, before Jason and Keri could be friends again, or Keri accept the new baby.

What all this means is that while you are trying to juggle who goes into which room and wondering how the children are going to cope with your new stepfamily, it might be worth stepping back a minute and actually looking at the patterns your new family might make. When you slot children together, will it give them a new and different place in the resulting family? How may that affect how they feel about themselves and you and how they react to others in the picture? Thinking about the Family Structure can certainly help you manage the new family far better.

Things to Keep in Mind

● Starting a stepfamily generally means squeezing more people – even if it's only one – into the same space. Territory tends to be important – think and talk over how you will deal with this.

● If there are two sets of children involved, be prepared for their attitudes to each other to be less consistent than those of the adults. They may swing from being total enemies to being best friends almost on a daily basis.

● If you've been a single parent you may have got used to operating as a tight little unit, together. You may have to make a conscious effort to start being a two-adult family again, and you may have to help your children adjust to this as well.

● Putting two sets of children together alters the age and status 'pecking order' for all of them. This could be fun – it could be trouble; talk it over with them.

● Look out for and actively encourage the potential plus points in bringing two sets of children together. An only child may acquire siblings, a middle child a same-age playmate, the baby of the family become a senior.

● Take the occasional step back and look at the pattern your new family is forming. Thinking objectively about the family's developing structure can help you manage it better.

Chapter 8

Grandparents and Other Relatives

When we think or talk about stepfamilies, we tend to think only of the people at the centre of the picture. We focus on the adults forming a new family, with the children of one of them who live there full-time, such as Chris and Tracie, with her children and theirs. Or we think about families such as Sharon's and Andy's, with children of both of them in full-time residence. Or Carlos and Fi, who see his children most weekends. We may recognize that for each stepfamily there must be satellite parents – the fathers of Tracie's children, Sharon's and Andy's exes and Carlos's ex-wife. What we often forget is that there are other people also caught up in both the break-up of the previous relationships, and the formation of the new ones. Grandparents, aunts and uncles, brothers and sisters and even adult children all play a role that is not simply that of being spectators. Their feelings are important and their actions highly significant to all concerned. You might have sorted out how you, your children and previous partners are going to manage this new family. If other members of your family aren't in agreement or on board you may find that their attitudes, beliefs and behaviour can scupper any hopes you have of plain sailing.

Grandparents often take on a vital protective role during family break-up. They may give the adults involved some **support and security**. But more importantly they often hold out to children the one stable point in a crumbling universe. Children who are losing their sense of certainty and security as they watch their parents' marriage and their family break down can at least be reassured that this part of their family remains intact. Grandparents may be boring and old-fashioned, and visits to them never vary – but that becomes an absolute virtue when everything else you hold dear in your life is changing all too much. Grandparents often become more and more central in a child's life when one parent is left on their own, stepping in to provide increasing levels of childcare. Children often turn to grandparents or aunts and uncles when they want someone they feel they can trust but who is outside the immediate family to talk to. And when one parent is permanently no longer on the scene because of a death, their relatives become a real anchor point in somehow keeping the link between children and their dead parent.

This is why it can destabilize and upset children so much when the bonds they have with grandparents and other family members begin to fray and come apart as their family alters. It was the absolute final straw for Amy, Vicky and Sam when their grandparents moved away and severed contact, on top of their losing dads and stepdads. And Daniel never saw his father's parents, although they sent Christmas cards. When a relationship comes to an end battle lines are often drawn. Many family members feel their place is defending their own family member against an ex-partner. In some families, this rule is broken, but not to be impartial. Instead, the family may turn on its own, accusing them of being the cause of or to blame for the break-up and siding with the other partner. This can particularly happen if separation is happening because of an affair or some other dispute. Or it may happen around the circumstances of a new relationship. A mum or dad, sister or brother who particularly liked their in-law may feel angry when a widow or widower decides life must go on and that they can't mourn a dead partner forever. They and the new partner may find the family expresses anger at the incomer by quarrelling with both of them. The problem is that relatives who want to cut off ties with an adult with whom they feel upset often forget that while they may be hurt or feel rejected by the action, the children caught in the crossfire feel that and more. The reasons for the quarrel go straight over their heads. All they know is that Auntie so-and-so or Grandpa obviously doesn't love them or want to know them any more. Dave and Laura lost their mother when they were around 7 and 5. Last summer, their mother's mother died. During the Easter break, their father's father and their mother's father died … and one of the family cats, a treasured companion, also died. To top it all, relations between their father and stepmother and their aunt and uncles on their mother's side were not good. It was as if the last links with the past and their mother were being cut one by one.

Sometimes the **loss of contact** is deliberate and planned. The relatives involved argue with the new couple and refuse to see them, and in doing so lose touch with the children. Or every time they do interact, it becomes so unpleasant that the couple or the kids feel they can't take it and cry off any further visits. But in other cases what happens is that visits or meetings simply fade away. This particularly happens with relatives from the side of the family that no longer has the children with them full-time – usually, the father's side. Steve's parents never stopped loving or wanting to see Rebecca and Ryan, but Steve and his daughter had a period of not being in touch. His parents felt unable to go directly to Rebecca's mother, Lynn, and so were unable to arrange to see their grandchildren independent of Steve. Contact with children is often mediated and arranged by mothers, or at least by the women involved, rather than by men. If it's the woman with whom there is a quarrel – as many parents of separated men see it – then there is no one looking out for, taking responsibility for and facilitating the continuing relationship between grandparent and grandchild. Even when there is no overwhelming hostility, awkwardness and hesitation may have the same affect. Contact, which the children may feel is important but the adults haven't realized is so fundamental, can be lost.

As far as children are concerned, a grandparent is a grandparent. Your dad's mum or your mum's dad – you can love them just as much and see very little difference. In many families, however, there may already be a distinction. Women tend to have closer ties to their parents than men do to theirs, and may already have enabled children to have a closer tie with Nan and Gramps than Grandma and Grandpa. But if children have made little disparity, it can be horribly unsettling to suddenly lose people who matter and not to know or understand why. All human beings search for meanings in situations, and children always have a tendency to blame themselves when something goes wrong. Instead of looking to the difficulties in communication between the adults, children may conclude that it's because they are unlovable, unworthy or bad that Gran and Grandad no longer stay in touch.

Sometimes what is happening is that the anger washing about in the family over the break-up can become focused on the new partner. They may be seen as being at fault over a break-up, even if in fact they arrived some time after that had happened. If this is patently nothing to do with them it may still be the focus of anger as being the reason why a reconciliation is no longer on the cards. But even when there is neither a break-up to lay at their feet or a chance of reconciliation – such as after a death – relatives may simply blame the new person for not being the missing person. Their grief and anger has to go somewhere, and the new member of the family seems to be the best target.

All this can be especially tough on an incomer who comes into family after an ex has left in bitterness and ill-will. For the sake of the children, you should be nice about the ex in front of the children and ease their seeing each other. On top of that, you have to do the same for that person's relatives, even if they seem to be stirring up arguments and bad-mouthing you. You may feel they have no rights at all and are an utter irrelevancy and wish to have done with them, for some peace and quiet. But for the children, keeping contact may be really important. Quite apart from the emotional fallout of losing touch with relatives, they provide a support network that you all may need.

When a family comes together, new arrivals may find themselves excluded and made to feel like trespassers by some relatives, who only want to acknowledge **blood ties**. Arguments often erupt between incoming adults and other relatives because of the way each sees the other's place in the family. Grandparents of the resident parent often feel they have more rights with the children than the incoming new adult, especially if they have had a caring role during or after a break-up. They may deeply resent the way a new partner assumes a certain caring role with the children. Caitlin's parents did not get on with Trevor when he first moved in. They clashed over rules and parenting styles, even when it became clear that Trevor loved Tamsin and Jonah and wanted to do his best by them. After the mistakes made at their first Christmas, Trevor tried very hard to get the various grandparents and other family on board. Caitlin's parents were deeply resistant, and what seemed to emerge is that they felt as if Trevor was taking something away from them by moving in and reading Jonah bedtime stories and taking Tamsin to her swimming club. Tamsin was worried about putting on weight and Trevor supported her in a healthy eating plan. Her grandmother saw this as a direct attack on her, and refused to stop giving them chips and other fried food when they came to stay. Such arguments can be even more bitter

Family Round Table

In the *Stepfamilies* TV series I asked some of the families to practise having family discussions – Family Round Tables. Adults sometimes use 'family discussions' as a way of telling children what they have decided to do. It isn't, however, a true Family Round Table unless all of you listen as much, if not more, than you talk and unless young people are given as much space and respect to have their say as are adults. A family parliament is an ideal way, not just of keeping in touch, but also of pulling everyone together. In a separated family, it really helps to make time and space for Family Round Tables regularly. You can do it with the family that lives together. But it also helps to make room for those who have contact but may not live together full-time.

The difference between a dictatorship and a democracy is the assembly. In the days when city states were small, all the members entitled to vote would come together to voice their opinions and vote. As populations became bigger, those with a vote would use it to put their choice of elected member into a senate or parliament, to discuss and legislate. You can run your family as a dictatorship, where only adults have a say, or you can claim you're presiding over a democracy where your kids are too young to be able to make choices. If you do, don't forget what usually happens in such systems. The oppressed peoples either overthrow the state in bloody revolution, or emigrate and never come back.

There are three main rules to make a family round table discussion work.

Equality

Everyone, from oldest to youngest, is to have an equal turn to speak and to be heard. You might like to go round the table letting each person say one thing, to start. Then, take turns to add to the discussion. You can use an object handed round to signify whose turn it is to speak. In the series, I gave each family a giant shell – a conch. Only the person holding the conch could speak, and handed it on when they were done. Ask everyone to keep the rule about only talking when they have had it handed on to them. It helps to appoint one person to act as the Facilitator for a Family Round Table, and to have each member of the group take it turn-and-turn-about to play this role. The facilitator ensures that everyone takes it in turns to speak and not interrupt.

Owning what you say

The most important rule is that everyone has to 'own' what they say. That means, everything you put forward has to be your own thoughts and feelings and you should acknowledge them as such, saying 'I think' or 'I feel'. No one can say 'So-and-so says' or 'Everyone knows' or talk about what other people do or what you think they think. You can talk about how other people's behaviour affects you, by saying, 'When you do such-and-such, I feel ...' but the aim is to put your point of view, not to criticize or attack other people. Remember, the key is confronting problems, not people.

Consensus

The eventual aim of your discussion is to find a space where everyone feels they have been heard and appreciated, and have heard and appreciated everyone else's point of view. There should be no winners or losers, but an all-round agreement on the outcome. To that end, no one is to be shouted down for what they say. Discuss the points rather than arguing with the person. Set aside time for the discussion and allow everyone a chance to speak, as many times as they like.

if it's their own role that the new adult is seen to be supplanting.

When a parent dies, their family may take greater offence over anything a new partner does than when it's after a divorce or separation. A new relationship may be seen as finally sweeping away all the memories and the last lingering presence of the loved one who is gone. Their grief may turn to anger, and be discharged on the incoming adult as if it was their fault the other parent is dead. When this happens and the family of a dead parent withdraws or becomes hostile, it can be especially hurtful for the children left behind. They have lost a mum or dad. Now they may have to stand by as the family of that parent becomes distant and unapproachable. It's not only a loss in itself – it's a further loss of the last remaining links with the parent they miss and mourn.

It may not be hostility that a new partner has to face but indifference. Grandparents and other relatives may reluctantly acknowledge that this new person has a relationship with the adult, but not want to accept they have any link with the children concerned, and thus with them. This lack of connection is particularly likely to be extended to new children, especially when these are weekend visitors. When Carlos married Fi, her mother made it clear that she felt his children had nothing to do with her. She was polite and asked after them – as Carlos's children, not as Fi's stepchildren. She never sent cards or presents on their birthday or at Christmas. As far as she was concerned, they had nothing to do with her. Over time, Fi made an extremely good relationship with them and came to see them as her own children, while they saw her as a special person in their lives. She rejoiced in their successes and supported them through hard times. But she soon found she simply couldn't discuss them or what she thought of as 'her' family with her mother. Fi's mother never accepted them as anything but an irrelevance, which Fi found sad and painful.

Birthdays and festivals are often the times when such gaps are most obvious, as some relatives treat one set of children differently from others. The first Christmas that Caitlin and Trevor shared was a nightmare. Her younger son, 8-year-old Jonah, had presents from his own father and his father's parents, as well as his grandparents on Caitlin's side. Trevor's son Connor had presents from him and Trevor's parents, and from his own mother and her parents. But Caitlin's daughter, 13-year-old Tamsin, has no contact with either her father or his parents. Her pile of presents was considerably smaller than the other two. Trevor's parents didn't feel that either of his new stepchildren were anything to do with them and didn't give either of them gifts. At least they were consistent in that, but it meant that Tamsin was the only one on Christmas Day with presents only from her Mum and stepfather. On top of that, Trevor had insisted that he and Caitlin spend exactly the same amount on all three, to be fair. But this didn't take into account the fact that toys for small children tend to be cheaper than the sort of things a 13-year-old likes. The same amount may have been spent but it resulted in far more parcels for Jonah and Connor – and it's parcels that children count, not price tags. Tamsin dissolved into tears, and then erupted in a screaming rage that didn't end until Boxing Day.

Of course, it isn't always easy to **maintain the links** between children and grandchildren if you don't live with them and only see your kids for a short time. When Carlos sees his children, he jealously guards the time he has with them and at first resented taking them to see his parents. Gradually he came to realize that they really needed that contact as well as contact with him. They got into the habit of popping by for Saturday breakfast, and the result was that eventually his children and their grandparents were able to organize their own time together, sometimes in the week and with Carlos's ex. She had got on well with her in-laws until the break-up, and one good spin-off of Carlos making this effort was that she renewed her relationship with them, too.

Carlos's ex had made no objections to his taking their children to see their paternal grandparents. Sometimes, the resident parent can be incensed when an ex has kids for access visits and takes them to see, and may even leave them with, other relatives. Trevor's ex was furious to hear he had taken Connor to see his parents and then gone shopping with his stepdaughter Tamsin. She believed that if Trevor wanted to see Connor, he should be spending time with him, not dumping him on his grandparents. What got lost in her anger was Connor's needs. What he needed most of all was seeing his grandparents as well as his father. But he also needed to see them in as natural a way as possible – in a way that underlined they were still a 'normal' family. And being dropped off to spend some time with them alone was most like the way he had seen them before the break-up. Such an arrangement best followed a normal weekend, and he liked it. When Trevor's ex finally recognized this, she was happy to help.

As the incoming adult to a stepfamily, you do need to recognize the importance of other family members to the children you are taking on. Billy found it difficult to get on with Adele's two sons from the beginning, even though they were happy to have him come and live with them. His entire focus was on his own children from a previous relationship and he made little effort to make any kind of relationship with his new partner's two boys. They finally gave him up as a bad job, and became downright hostile to him, when their grandfather – their father's father – died. They had kept in touch with him, one of the few members of their family they still saw and were close to. His death was a terrible blow to them … and Billy hardly acknowledged it. As far as he was concerned, the father of the man he had replaced was irrelevant to him, and he didn't see or want to see how important he was to them.

What is obviously important is for there to be **communication**, among couples, between parents who no longer live together, between family members. Adults need to listen to children and to each other, and to take on board the anger and hurt and guilt all may be feeling and find a way round them. Kids can be devastated by a breakdown in family ties. Of course some

Family History

Children love hearing about family history. They love stories about themselves when they were young, about parents and especially about grandparents. When a child first asks, 'Where do babies come from?' they are not really enquiring about biology or sex. What they actually are wondering is where they came from, whether the world existed before they came into being and their place within it. With family change there is often a gap. Children lose the secure pattern of their family as it was. But children can cope with something new as long as they have the safe foundation of what was there before. The big problem is that the changes may be so painful that large areas of their past, present or future life become taboo. Children don't only lose their family as it was; they lose the experience of being able to talk about it. They lose their history and their identity.

One way we confirm a shared family history is to talk about it, passing on stories about the things we or relatives have done.

Another way is to look at photographs or videos, which show the past. New families often become awkward about doing these, because it feels as if you only underline difference when one part of the family talks about a history which doesn't 'belong' to another part or looks at pictures that show missing relatives. New members may feel at a disadvantage and fear comparisons. Old members may think stirring up the past will only make them depressed. Far from underlining loss or creating resentment, thinking and talking about the past can only be helpful. If you try to pretend nothing existed before your present family structure, you live a lie which makes it difficult to develop a future form. Far better to use photos, stories and even a family tree to show how the past still lives, but has transformed into the family you now have. Encourage your wider family to give your children and stepchildren a sense of belonging and of their continuing story, by telling them family stories.

may be relieved, if the relatives in question hadn't made a good bond with them – it's a good excuse to no longer have to see tedious or bitchy Aunt Agnes! But however boring or difficult you may feel they are, family are family and can be important. It's up to all the adults involved in a family break-up and in new families to be grown-up and do what's best for the children. And what is best for them is communication and friendship, not distance and hostility.

One other aspect to pay attention to might the legal one. When a child comes into a family by being a stepchild, even if their parent marries the new partner, this does not mean they acquire legal title with other members of that family. Stan adored the children his daughter Leah gained by marrying Abe. Little Abe and Naomi became as precious to him as his full blood-related grandchildren. When he died, he had intended them to be as much recipients of his legacy as the others, and left an equal amount of money to 'all my grandchildren'. Sadly, in law, they were nothing of the kind. They were given the specific things he had named as going to each child, but the actual estate he'd left to be divided up among eight children was given to six – the direct line descendants, excluding Abe's children, Leah's stepchildren. If Stan had named his six grandchildren and two stepgrandchildren in his will, or specified he'd meant his stepgrandchildren as well, his wishes would have been honoured.

Of course, many grandparents and other relatives are able to recognize the roots of any resentment and anger and put them aside for the sake of the children. It often helps for exes to get together, maybe with the help of a counsellor or mediator, to finish the argument, thrash out problems and work out ways of working together as co-parents. In the same way, it might help some families to do the same. New couples may find it useful to invite relatives together when they decide to set up home, to explain what is going on, to ask for support and invite discussion. Introducing the new adult as someone who wants to do their best and who'd appreciate support may prevent rumours and gossip.

Things to Keep in Mind

- Relatives on both sides may be forgotten or miss out in the confusion surrounding the start of a new stepfamily. But if family members are not on board, their attitudes, beliefs or behaviour can make life difficult.

- Grandparents can be a child's best protection and givers of stability when a family breaks up or a new stepfamily forms.

- Women are often the ones to keep contact between children and relatives going. If Mum isn't prepared to make that effort, contacts can lapse.

- Newcomers can become the focus of relatives' anger even when they had nothing to do with the original break-up. It's nothing personal. The grief and anger has to go somewhere and the new partner is the best and easiest target.

- To many people 'blood links' are still the most important. This can mean that in a new stepfamily a new partner may be accepted by relatives or friends, but any children he or she brings with them may still be felt to be outsiders.

- It's important to separate any lingering anger you still have for other adults from your dealings with the children involved. Put aside those arguments to let children see the people they value, even if you don't get on with them.

- Celebrate and continue to discuss your family history. Encourage relatives to tell your children and indeed your stepchildren the stories about your family that children enjoy hearing and need to hear.

Chapter 9

Two Households

When stepfamilies are in crisis, most of the children, and some of the adults, will survey the scene and say they wish they could be a 'normal' family. A normal family, they seem to be saying, is one like their friends have, where people seldom argue. Jas wished her brother Sean and her stepmother wouldn't always bicker, and said she particularly liked visiting her father because it was quiet – 'No arguments. And when I visit my friends, it's nice too. They don't have rows all the time. I wish we could be like them.'

The level of conflict in stepfamilies can be felt to be unusual and unlike that in 'normal' families. However, what you see from the outside may not be what happens on the inside. Parents and children in first-time families argue and disagree just as much as those in stepfamilies. The real difference between first-time and stepfamilies is not conflict but shape. Stepfamilies stand out and seem different because people live apart – one parent from the other, children from one parent. Children find themselves never seeing their birth dad or mum, or seeing them part-time or irregularly. Children divide their time between homes, and may find it hard to know where they are or be able to invite friends over because of this. And that is what makes it feel so *not* 'normal'. Yet it's possible to dredge some advantages up from living in two households, it just takes some work and understanding on the part of all the adults and children involved.

In fact, rows are often what a 'normal' family is all about – having conflicts and disagreements and variations in opinion and needs. This can happen in first-time families that stick together as well as those that come apart and then become second-time families. The difference between a happy family and an unhappy one is not that you argue but how you resolve such arguments. Families that function well do so because they deal with their disagreements. They talk them through and they give support, respect and a listening ear to everyone in the family, and everyone who may be important to the family but be living elsewhere. When children say they would like their family to be 'normal', what they are expressing is the pain they feel at seeing their family change, hurt at losing the security and certainty that having a mum and dad at home can bring. Quarrels and continuing friction only make it worse. Their complaint and wish is that this could be brought under some sort of control. Helping children – and adults! – to see that families do come in all shapes and sizes, and can work even when they seem to go against the norm, is the answer. And the truth is that over the next few years we will see the family norm shift from being a first-time family of two parents living with their children towards all sort of different varieties of household. Your stepfamily will be as 'normal' as any other.

Having two households, however, means having to make some effort to make it work. Children clearly benefit from contact with both parents, even if it means dividing their time between two homes, whether on a regular basis or for occasional weekends and holidays. The adults with whom children live full-time often have reservations about such contact. You may feel the ex-partner has already failed as a partner or now makes children unhappy or difficult by seeing them. However, what you think of your children's, or your stepchildren's, other parent may have very little resemblance to what they think. Even a poor excuse for a mum or dad, someone you feel is never there for them or who rejects or even ill-treats them, is still their parent; someone they love and need.

They need them because we get our picture of who we are, and what we are, from our parents. We are made of a half and half mix of both mother and father. And we acquire our feelings of self, of worthiness and acceptability and esteem from that relationship. When a parent turns their back on us or tells or demonstrates to us that they don't want to know, we assume it's our fault and that the reason they left was because we didn't measure up. Children with such a belief can grow up severely lacking in confidence and self-worth. Whatever you think of the other parent, whatever your experience of them, it may be vitally important for your children for you to make it as easy as possible for them to retain a relationship and as much contact as possible. The amount of time they spend with each of you isn't a prize or a badge that says you do it best. Tim, for instance, seemed to feel that if his stepchildren wanted to or did spend time with their father, it diminished him. Of course, time isn't infinite and a day spent with one person means a day less with the other. But quality time with a happy child is worth far more than depriving a child of something they need.

But children can feel confused going from one home to another unless the situation is carefully managed. I have already touched on the way unfinished business from the past can affect your relationship with your ex and your present partner, and the children. The way you manage, or fail to manage, living in two households is where these issues often raise their ugly heads.

Family Rules

In the TV series I asked all the stepfamilies to come up with a set of House or Family Rules. I did this for several reasons.

For a start, every family does and should have some rules they live by. Sometimes, these have been discussed and everyone knows them. Sometimes, they're sort-of known and sort-of agreed. Often they do exist but people aren't always sure what they are exactly and they do change from time to time. Putting together a set of Family or House Rules means you have to discuss them, agree them and learn what they are. Then there's no excuse for not realizing what you should or should to be doing.

The second reason I ask every family to set rules is that when people in the stepfamily want to make a point or kick off or be uncooperative, the first thing they usually say is: 'You can't tell me what to do, you're not my mum/dad!' Having House or Family Rules bypasses that. There should be no rudeness, no disrespect, no hitting or shouting or slamming doors or whatever you have all agreed. And that's not because some big bad adult has tried to usurp a parent's place and is telling you what to do; it's because that's the House rule, and you all keep it.

By talking the rules through and allowing everyone to have their say, you get two results. One is that everyone should 'buy in to' the rules. You set them, you had a chance to make them or alter them, now you keep them. And this means all members of the house get a say – kids too. For every rule that the adults want, there should be one the children put forward. For instance, in Carlos and Fi's household there were rules about not swearing and shouting or hitting. But there was also a rule that said the children could choose a game to play every Sunday night – Monopoly, Cluedo, Scrabble, whatever – and the adults had to take part. And that in the first ten minutes when the children arrived for a visit, Carlos and Fi had to sit and listen to what had happened to them since they were last there.

Another result of talking through the rules is that setting them helps young people as well as adults think about why they are needed and what might be the effect of having – or not having – them. Sometimes, it helps adults realize priorities. After all, does it really matter if a child's room is untidy? Surely having sensible times for them to come home, or go to bed, are more important. And if you kick up a major fuss over the less important things, you lose out on being able to say, 'No, this one really IS important.' Discussing rules allows you to choose your battles. And you'll be surprised how sensible young people can be, given the responsibility and the option. But perhaps the number one result of having a say in what should be the rules in a stepfamily is that it allows you all to feel a part of this house – to have a place and a stake in it. This can be vitally important in a stepfamily household.

You set House or Family Rules by all getting together round a table with a big sheet of paper and some pens. This is the preliminary stage – you're not looking for perfection or neatness at this point. Appoint someone to be the note-taker. And then Ideas Storm.

Ideas Storming is putting down EVERYTHING that comes to mind. Ask, 'What House or Family Rules do we think we already have? What House or Family Rules do we want?' You might also ask, 'What problems do we have and how could we do something about them?'

Write down every single suggestion. Even if you think them unworkable, silly, too difficult to manage. The only thing you should exclude might be rules that anyone suggests with the intention of 'getting at' another member of the family. So 'No coming in and messing up my books' when only one other child does so may be a bit barbed. But 'Everyone to ask before using anyone else's belongings' is fair – it applies to all.

Having written everything down, the second stage; look at and consider them. Think about what you all want to achieve. Some of your rules may be about getting on with each other – about being nice and helpful. You might put in a rule about not swearing, hitting, fighting, shouting. Some may be about running the home smoothly – you might have a family rule about always taking shoes off at the door, or always hanging coats up when you come in or always washing up your own coffee cups. Some may be about big and important things such as teenagers always carrying mobiles when they're out at night with friends and never getting into a car with a driver who's been drinking.

Third stage is agreeing which rules you will choose to be your House or Family Rules. You might like to rewrite rules to make them as constructive as possible – that is, use 'Dos' rather than 'Don'ts'. Be as specific as possible – a vague rule about respecting people is less helpful that saying people should listen to each other, not shout them down, interrupt or call them names. You may find you have some overlapping rules – prune or combine them. You may have some you don't like, and some the children don't like. Make your case and listen to theirs. And do some 'Horse Trading' – this rule stays in if I say yes to that one.

Then, write them out neatly. Agree you will all keep them – you might like to draw up a contract that says so, and ALL (adults included) sign it. Hang up the House or Family Rules and the contract somewhere you can all see them.

Revisit them regularly – maybe once a week. Are they working? If not, why not? What needs to be changed?

When two parents live apart, their relationship is generally held to be over. But while you may no longer be partners, you are still parents and a separation or divorce can never end that part of your responsibility – your **shared responsibility**. The trick is to accept that your private, one to one, couple bond may be gone but your bond as co-parents remains. Co-parenting means both of you communicating and agreeing on the basics – singing from the

Here are some rules you might consider – these are the ones Caitlin, Trevor, Tamsin, Jonah and Connor agreed:

- Shoes off at the door and always hang coats up.

- If you have a snack, wash up after yourselves.

- Do your chores with no arguments.

- Talk with each other instead of shouting at each other.

- No kicking, hitting, shoving, biting, swearing or shouting.

- Be kind, be positive, praise often and always say Please, Thank You and Well Done.

- If you want someone to hear you, you have to listen to them.

- Help people do better instead of criticizing them to bring them down.

- Have a family talk at least once a week.

- Go out as a family at least once a month.

- Go to bed at agreed times.

- Do homework at the beginning of a night or weekend.

- Pocket money to be given every Friday night.

- The more chores you do, the more pocket money you earn.

- Say what time you'll be home and keep to it – that applies to you, too, Trevor!

same song-sheet, in effect. But it doesn't have to mean always doing things the same way. Geoff and Sandy, for instance, have different rules and expectations of their children and on the surface seem to be operating very different parenting styles and homes. Geoff believes in talking things through and in children having a say; Sandy is more traditional and inclined to make decisions and expect her children to respect her views and follow her requests.

Bedtime at Geoff's is half an hour later than at Sandy's. This could, in some families, cause problems. Paul strongly feels his partner Joanne's ex, Simon, deliberately lets his children get away with murder when they're with him and encourages them to challenge Paul in his home. They come home full of 'Dad says this, Dad says that, Dad lets us, you can't tell us …' The different styles are in conflict because the children can't keep them apart. Sally says her ex, Daniel, refuses to discuss or negotiate agreements or shared rules and expectations they might have of their daughter Dee. Sally has particular health concerns that need to be settled – Dee has asthma and Sally says she comes back smelling of cigarette smoke because Daniel and his girlfriend smoke and continue to do so when she's with them. Sally says when she tries to discuss this with Daniel he tells her it is none of her business what happens in his home and when he is with his children. Andy also will not talk to his ex, Kerry, about their children – he insists that anything she gave them for Christmas must stay with her, for when they visit her; and makes the same insistence for anything Sharon's ex, Michael, or their grandparents give to Josh and Rhiannon. According to Andy, what he does is his business in his family.

Geoff and Sandy, however, both agree to differ, and say so to their children. It's understood that bedtimes and how discussions are managed are different and agreed to be so; the rule is, what happens in one house belongs to that house and there are no disputes about it. Children can manage this variation when it's explained and agreed. After all, it's the way things happen in the wide world; what you do at home is different from the way you do it at school. What Geoff and Sandy always keep to is to talk over what would be shared decisions, such as to do with school or holidays. They keep each other updated on whatever they do with their children and their children tell each of them. Both care deeply for their children and respect the other one and their part in their children's lives. Tim, Lynn and Steve arrived at the same conclusion. After some pain and difficulties, they took the heroic step of all meeting up for a discussion. The upshot was that they also now communicate and agree. Until that happened, Tim had felt Ryan's father, Steve, would send him back primed to say, 'You're not my father'. He thought this was a direct result of Steve's influence because Ryan always used to say it after visits to his Dad. The level of hostility was so great that Steve would refuse to discuss what happened when Ryan was with him, saying it was none of Tim and Lynn's business what happened in his home.

It's a difficult trick to master, but the fact is that while you may no longer be partners, you are still both equal parents to your children, even if one takes on full-time care and the other only sees them for short periods. As far as the children are concerned, you both fulfil the role of their full-time parents, even if one of you does not function as a full-time carer. You may live separately and one of you may have sole residency of the children. Unless it has been taken away by the courts, you still **share parental responsibility**. Parental responsibility recognizes that both parents are vital to children. You affect your child's upbringing, well-being and both physical and emotional health, however often you actually see them face to face or talk or otherwise communicate with them. You are a continuing presence in their lives, even if you hardly ever or never see them. If you can't agree to co-parent in some way, your children suffer. Your ex-partner suffers too, and that may be your intention. But they won't be the only one doing so. Which is why it's so important to understand what a child means when they come home from a visit bristling and ready to cry, 'You can't tell me what to do, you're not my dad,' or 'Mum says I can …' While children may be able to cope with different parenting styles and house rules, parents who use the differences to attack each other can leave them feeling anxious and caught in the middle between parents scoring points.

Children can manage the differences between households, but not if you use them against each other. They can also manage having two bases, but only if both feel like home. I will hold my hands up at this point. When my stepson was young, he would visit for some weekends and holidays. But he was an occasional visitor – he didn't come every weekend and he didn't come for all of the holidays. So when choosing a home, we went for an inner-city one-bedroom flat rather than looking further out for a two-bedroom one – after all, he wasn't with us that often. Big mistake. My stepson never really felt he was a proper part of our lives, with a stake and a place in our home. He was a visitor, sleeping on a put-up bed. Children who visit their non-residential parent, however fleetingly and irregularly, desperately need to feel they belong, that they have roots in that home. If you can't give them a bedroom, give them a corner. If you can't give them a corner, give them a chest of drawers or a box or a drawer that is theirs, in which they can leave stuff to come back to. My stepson used to start every visit by going round the flat, checking up on what was still there and what might have arrived or gone missing. He was like a cat checking out the territory to see if it was still familiar. Children need their territory, and their markers.

The other important issue is that visiting, even if it is to somewhere that feels like a home to them, underlines the fact that one of their parents lives away. The more comfortable they feel there and the more secure they are in returning when they choose, the less

Family Answering Machine Message

You may not have an answering machine – in lots of families now everyone has their own mobiles, and there may not even be a fixed phone in the house. But if you do, does the message reflect everyone in the house, even those who stay a short time? It may seem trivial, but knowing you are part of the message and it says you belong and spend time there can often be immensely reassuring for a child who may be feeling insecure or left out. Get your family together and create a message that names everyone and invites messages to be left for all of them.

this may hurt. But the very nature of such visits – that they are visits to someone they by rights should have living with them – means they come back feeling miserable, hurt, angry and perhaps guilty. And they need to express these feelings, often in anger and blame and rejection – to match up with exactly how much anger, fault and rejection they are feeling. So they hit out – and often the easiest target to hit at is the stepparent, who is seen as the author of all the troubles. And the parent with whom they live full-time, who they trust to never leave them. The parent they visit doesn't have to, doesn't need to, 'set them up' to be challenging to the stepparent or the full-time parent. It is their own feelings of confusion, loss and rage that do that.

Parents sometimes make it hard for their children for two reasons. One is that they feel they are in a contest, a **tug-of-love** for their children's allegiance. Parents cling to their own different parenting styles and household atmospheres and instead of concluding: 'Well, that's how it is with us and what does it matter how the other place is?' they begin feeling: 'I want to be loved best, so I want the way we do things to be seen as the best.' Parents may then set themselves up in competition, unable to recognize that different parenting styles are just that – the way the other parent does it. Instead, it becomes a direct attack on them, their beliefs, their way of life. And parents may even start encouraging behaviour they would recognize is unhelpful for the child – late nights, unhealthy foods, unsuitable videos or games – in an attempt either to win favour, or to annoy the other household. Or indeed, it may seem to one parent that the other one is doing that ... when it may not be so. As I've already said, when a child comes home spitting with anger and blame at a stepparent or resident parent, it may have nothing to do with your having been bad-mouthed in the other household. And when your child says 'Dad lets me ...' or 'When I'm with Mum we ...' it doesn't always mean what they say is the truth. Very few children are above using your separated status to get a rise. Sometimes they really have misinterpreted or misunderstood what is going on, and what they say to you is inaccurate. But sometimes they are deliberately exaggerating for their own ends. After all, if you get upset about being told it's all pizza and ice cream and late night films for all they know you're not going to be on the phone to sound off; you're going to try to offer one better. What child can resist that?

Children whose parents live away from them do realize they have some handy buttons to push. You may suffer terrible guilt and yearning over the separation, and long to make up for it. This is how Trevor felt at first about his son Connor, who lived mainly with his mother. The result was that Trevor tried to spend as much time with Connor as he could when he was with him, and tried to make that time special. He was too young to do chores, he felt, and when he misbehaved he hadn't the heart to tell him off. The trouble was that his favouritism couldn't go unnoticed by his stepchildren, who felt both rejected in comparison and resentful.

It's often very important for children to have some control over the process of **access and visits**. Visits can be soured, for instance, if you and their other parent gaily agree that little Johnny needs to see his dad this week and fail to realize that a vitally important party or gathering is going on. Children need to see both of their parents but they also need to be a part of their own social group and not miss out. It doesn't need to be an event you see as important for them to feel left out if they miss it, or for them to be excluded by the group if they don't turn up. Children also need to have some clear idea of what may be on the cards – when they can go, when a parent may not be available. Once Steve, Tim and Lynn and their now shared children Ryan and Rebecca had sorted out their differences, they took my advice in coordinating their schedules. Steve's parents bought Ryan, Rebecca and Steve diaries and with the help and cooperation of Tim and Lynn they now keep these in line so everyone knows who is free when and which weekends they can and may not be able to see each other. Geoff and Sandy bought their children mobile phones with the agreement that while calls and texts with friends came out of pocket money, calls between the kids and their parents were 'free'. This means the children feel able to ring up and chat with the parent they're not with at the time, any time. They are also able to make their own arrangements for visits, a vital factor to feeling more in control.

One aspect of the two households that can be less than helpful is that for what seem perfectly practical reasons, women tend to be the ones looking after the children in both homes. So, children living with their mum and stepfather may actually find it quite hard to establish a relationship with him, because it's always Mum with whom they interact. When Chris and his stepchildren were arguing, Tracie would intervene and smooth things out. Which might have made for an immediate solution, but in the long run prevented them from being able to sort anything out between themselves or coming to any understanding of what was going on and why. The same thing happened between Denise, Ian and his stepchildren. But it also happens when children are with their own father, whether full-time or part-time. Caitlin had become the one who looked after the physical and emotional well-being of Connor, even though he was her stepchild. When Trevor was late home from work it fell to her to be the one talking with, caring for, being there for Connor. What this meant was that Trevor, like many fathers, could actually evade either responsibility for or even knowledge of how difficult the situation might have become. Fathers often do say they never realized how bad things had got, until a crisis really did blow up in their faces.

The good news about having two households is that it can work, and can actually bring extra value. If children feel at home in both places, it can give them some variety and change. Every child has moments when the family they live in full-time can feel like a hothouse and they long to get away to a place where yesterday's argument isn't an issue. Having two homes also can bring new ideas, different viewpoints, a variety of tastes and traditions. Rebecca has found the joys of having two dads – Dad and Daddy. Each values her, each loves her and, now that they communicate and respect each other, both combine to give her and her brother the best of both worlds. And having children visit their other parent can give the adults in a stepfamily valuable breathing space. Most families long for time off to be a couple but simply can't afford the childcare; Sharon and Andy have every other weekend entirely on their own as their children go off to stay with their respective other parent. In a separated family each child has at least three adults if not four who can care and be on call – their two parents and their new partner(s). And if the missing parent has died, a stepparent may not be able to replace them but can fill some of the gap.

Things to Keep in Mind

● Communicate – with the other parent, with your partner, with the children. And that means listen as well as talk.

● If you still feel you and the other parent have issues, talk them through and put them aside.

● Agree to differ on some things. Different rules in different households can be fine as long as you're not working against each other.

● Agree some basics – safety issues such as calling home to say where you are and what time you'll be back.

- Include children in making arrangements.

- Recognize the only difference between stepfamilies and 'normal' families is shape. Conflict, arguments and differences are not unique to the stepfamily state, all families have them.

- The difference between a happy family, of whatever kind, and an unhappy one is not that they argue or have problems but how they resolve these.

- Children going from one home to another can feel confused and rootless unless the situation is managed very carefully – it's important for them to leave stuff behind and feel they have a base.

- You may no longer be partners but you're still co-parents. A separation or a divorce can never end that part of your relationship.

- As co-parents, discuss and agree on the basics of dealing with the children right from the beginning. The two of you singing from the same song sheet will get the best results for everyone.

- Children moving between two households will have some very handy emotional buttons to press with the adults involved. The more you are in touch with each other and cooperating, the less you can be manipulated.

Chapter 10

Losing Touch

Non-residential parents, particularly fathers, often lose touch with their children after a split, and especially after a new family is established. Some figures suggest as many as one in two will no longer be seeing their children after two years of separation. Joanne, for instance, had to watch her sisters Becky and Kat and her brother Tristan have regular contact with their father while hers was not in touch at all. Amy and Victoria hadn't been in touch with their father Darren for some time – he had felt he was doing the right thing in cutting off communication. Sam's father Andy is in touch, but usually irregularly and infrequently.

Why is it so important for children and parents who no longer live with them to keep in touch? Children learn about themselves and build up their self-image through the relationship they have with parents. In effect, they learn who they are by being with you – or by not being with you. They sometimes learn things that are less than helpful, sometimes things that will hardly stand them in good stead throughout life. A quote I have seen attributed to Dorothy Law Nolte puts the differences in the way children are treated and what they learn from it very well:

A child who lives with *criticism* learns to *condemn*.

A child who lives with *hostility* learns to *fight*.

A child who lives with *ridicule* learns to be *shy*.

A child who lives with *shame* learns to feel *guilty*.

A child who lives with *tolerance* learns to be *patient*.

A child who lives with *encouragement* learns *confidence*.

A child who lives with *praise* learns to *appreciate*.

A child who lives with *fairness* learns *justice*.

A child who lives with *security* learns *faith*.

A child who lives with *approval* learns to *like* themselves.

A child who lives with *acceptance* & *friendship* learns to find *love* in the world.

But it's not just how you bring up your children that affects them. Having both parents there is also profoundly important. Children know very well that they are the product of two parents and that some of both of you is in them and goes to make up their bodies and their personalities too. If children lose one parent, it feels like losing part of yourself, and leaves a father or mother shaped hole in their lives, which they may try to fill with guesses and fantasy. The **missing parent** may become a saint – and they may then believe it was their own fault in being not good enough that led to the parent going. Or they may see them as bad and awful in deserting them – and then that means part of them must be bad and awful, as it comes from them. Children may feel they cannot trust one or both parents, or any adult, for letting this happen. Or they may feel they cannot trust themselves, for being so unacceptable that the parent left them. Boys growing up without a father may feel they have to be extra male – and that often translates as extra aggressive, selfish, demanding – in order to fill the place left by the man in their lives. And girls may think they have to be extra female – and that can translate as extra sexy and precocious – to replace the missing father later in life. Both sexes can suffer from not having their own mother or father to identify with or learn from as they grow up. The good news is that you don't have to share a home to be fully in their lives. But you do have to maintain regular, consistent, predicable contact. Sadly, many parents not living with their children do find this hard.

In the majority of cases it is because contact is a painful, awkward, artificial experience. Tim stopped seeing his son Matthew when he was very small because the child slept through most visits. Tim was convinced it was because his ex kept Matthew awake deliberately, but he may simply not have realized how much small children do sleep, and he lost heart. Sometimes, resident parents tie access into maintenance. The line of reasoning may be: 'You can see your child if you pay on time but if you don't pay up, you can't see them.' A father who does not feel he is getting anything out of the contact, or getting headaches and grief, may back off at that point saying: 'Fine by me!'

Older children will often be moody before, truculent during and upset after a contact visit. Most parents with a co-parent who lives somewhere else will be familiar with the routine. For the resident parent, on the day of a visit beginning the child may be distracted and tense. They may be packing their stuff hours before, or leaving it until the very last moment. They may be hanging around the door gagging to go – or kicking their heels upstairs in their room, seemingly putting off the moment. Carlos and Fi sometimes dreaded the first few hours of his children's visits. The children would be quiet and glum and would often resist any attempts at cheering them up or getting them involved. Then, they'd usually perk up and be relaxed and happy and affectionate. And two or three hours before their return home, they'd switch off again. According to their mother, on return home they'd be argumentative and sometimes angry and tearful and at one point she considered stopping visits, saying it only seemed to upset them.

Both parents often do take from these sorts of reactions the idea that less contact would be better, and believe the child 'would be better off' without it. Vic and his partner Marian hardly ever see two of his children. His eldest son is banned from their house, after 'kicking off' one too many times and, as they saw it, causing rows between them and Marian's children. One of his daughters has sworn never to see them again and Vic's ex has said she'd prefer that, as the girl would go home after every visit in tears and raging. Vic says that if seeing him is so awful for them, it would be better if they kept away.

In fact, it's not that children hate seeing the parent they go to see. What they hate is the fact that it is a visit, not a return to home. The child is reacting to the nature of the situation; a contact stay underlines that at the end of the day or weekend, they or the parent goes away again. You're spending time with them, as if the parent and they are strangers, casual acquaintances, distant relatives, not a family. Visits make them feel as if their parent does not have a full-time presence in their life, which is the real thing they are objecting to in the only way they may know how.

Losing touch frequently happens because fathers are unable to carry on a relationship with a child if it isn't mediated by their partner, the child's mother. In many families, it's often Mum who 'does emotions'. Many fathers, in effect, carry on their relationships with their children through their partners. They may play football with them, but it's the women who remind them about birthdays, outings, what's going on and what's important in their children's lives. Once that relationship breaks down, so too does the link with the child. It can go on as before if the mother is determined to keep it going, or the child old enough and determined enough to make their own contact. But when the mother is angry and the children either too young to manage on their own or keen to please Mum, it may very well founder. The relationship may revive or be strengthened with a new partner, the stepmum, who may encourage and support it – or form her own friendship, as did Fi with Carlos's children.

But sometimes the parent losing touch will make little effort to keep the link, in the belief that they can go back later and take up where they have left off. Lee had had two children by two mothers when he met Carly. Both relationships had ended badly and Lee had stopped seeing his children, one when a baby and another when she was six. He felt he had been the victim in both arguments, and that his children would realize this when they grew up and would come looking for him, eager to hear his side of the story. Carly helped him see it a different way. He came to accept that arguments need two and that both he and his former partners would have contributed to what went wrong. Both had equal responsibility for keeping contact, and perhaps for remaking it. But most painfully and significantly, Carly helped Lee see that children cannot be put on hold. Adults may lose touch with friends and be able to slip back into the friendship as if no time had passed. Children can't.

Don't Argue – Communicate

There's nothing wrong with having a disagreement. The problems arise when it just leads to shouting, anger and further confusion. The trick is to make sure you are being heard and that you make yourself clear. Try these guidelines:

- Learn how to say 'I'. It's supposed to be arrogant or selfish to use the 'I' word so we tend to be brought up to avoid it. When we want to make a point, in discussion or argument, we either claim 'Everyone' or 'All my friends' or 'Your mother' thinks so and so, rather than taking responsibility for those feelings ourselves. Or we put the responsibility on the other person, by saying 'Look what you make me do.' One important step to constructive arguing is owning, or taking responsibility for, our own feelings. There is a great difference in saying, 'I'm angry because when you talk about your past I feel second best to your ex,' instead of: 'You make me feel second best!' The main difference is that the other person may rightly object to the second statement because it may not be their intention at all, and once they disagree you will find yourself stuck in the circular argument. But no one can disagree with an honest explanation of your own feelings. And once they are explained, you may be well on your way to dealing with them.

- Confront problems, not people. When you feel upset, stop to work out exactly what is bothering you. Instead of shouting at the person, explain what your anger or upset is really about, then find a way of agreeing on a resolution.

- Accept that you can't help what you feel. As we have already discussed, anyone in a second family is likely to have a complex and mixed range of feelings about themselves, the other people involved and the situation. Perhaps one of the most important messages we need to take on board is that those feelings, however destructive they are and however much they may distress you, are likely to be natural and normal. If you want to become comfortable with yourself and to reach a working arrangement with everyone else, the first step is to recognize and understand why you feel the way you do. So accept your feelings, even if they are sometimes ones you would rather not own to. Be honest about what you are feeling and why. You are not to blame for your emotions.

- Accept that you can help what you do about your feelings. You're being dishonest if you say you can't control your actions. Having gained some insight into why your circumstances might be so difficult, you can pinpoint your own fears, angers or anxieties. You can understand how the other people involved might feel, and work on strategies for making a change. Sometimes a 'pre-emptive strike' can nip problems in the bud before they really begin. Many families that experience change go through difficult periods but come out the other side, so don't despair. There are many things you can all do to improve your life together.

Children have quite short memory spans, perhaps because they do not have the experience that tells them someone will come back. Instead, they lose the image of a person in their minds the longer the real person remains away. And when it is a missing parent, they also tend to seek a reason why the breakdown in contact has happened. They may come to blame the parent, taking their cue from the angry or hurt parent they live with, and utterly reject or repudiate any attempt at later communication. More distressing, they may come to blame themselves, believing they are unworthy or bad and that this is the reason the parent left.

When the missing parent tries to remake the relationship, the child feels so confused and hurt that they cannot or will not accept the reconnection. Unlike adults, who may be able to accept the idea of postponement and delay, children need regular, constant, consistent contact. Barry was cavalier about his contact with his children. He loved them and they knew that, he said. So the fact that he called off half his agreed visits at the last moment should mean nothing – he'd see them eventually and what did it matter? It did matter – desperately. At first, his children would wait anxiously for him to arrive and be tearful and sad when he didn't show. Gradually, they stopped trusting him and stopped waiting for him. Eventually, they said they'd had enough; they didn't want to go through the lottery every weekend of would he/wouldn't he turn up, of getting excited and looking forward to seeing him only to be let down. Barry was taken aback – surely they knew it wasn't his fault? And maybe it was his ex who had 'got to them' and made them refuse to see him. He just couldn't accept that it was his own lack of commitment and understanding of their needs that led to them refusing to see him. Barry could not see that You Cannot Put Children On Hold.

Fathers may not appreciate what they've got in their children until it is too late and they lose them in a separation or divorce. Some fathers only

Draw up a Contract

Having had your talk, you need a clear way of keeping track of what you agreed needed changing and how you've agreed to go about it. To do that, you should draw up a contract.

Drawing up a contract

The idea is to write down exactly what everyone has said they will do. The key is that it shouldn't be one-sided, with one person or a few people asked to make an effort or making changes and other people acting as usual. Work out a fair exchange and one you can all agree. Make a precise record, including:

- what you've all agreed to do
- how you agree to do it
- when you agree to do it by
- for how long you have agreed to do this

Everyone should sign the contract, and have a copy for themselves. The original should be pinned up in your kitchen or hallway.

Follow up

Review the contract and the agreed changes regularly. If the terms are not being met, discuss why and whether the contract needs to be redrawn or whether something needs to be adjusted.

There are several very good spin-offs to this form of discussion. One is that it means you no longer have to be – you no longer should be – in the position of policing your family. If any of the children in your family have an argument, they should bring it to the round table discussion. But it's their responsibility, not yours, to sort it out. If a child and an adult have a disagreement, it's up to those involved to settle it. This puts a stop to Mum feeling she has to mediate between Dad and his children, when he should be having his own dialogue with them. Or one parent having to be the one who puts their foot down while the other gives all the treats. Another benefit is that if agreed changes are not fulfilled, everyone has the right to insist they must be.

galvanize themselves into being hands-on fathers, wanting to see their kids and be there for them, once they no longer actually live with them. This is why it's not a good idea for other relatives to point to a past poor performance and claim it as a reason to deny access. Leopards do change their spots, sometimes. Carlos says he thinks he is a good father – flexible, loving, supportive and available for his children and respectful of their needs. When he lived with them, he hardly listened to them and thought his work was far more of a priority. When he and his ex first parted, she was urged by her family to deny Carlos access, since he'd been so awful to her and to them. Fortunately, she recognized that someone can be a bad partner but a good parent. Whatever had happened between them, it was over and could and should be laid to rest. Their children deserved a second chance at having the father they wanted and needed, and that Carlos now wanted and needed to be. Since his separation, Carlos has never missed a visit, nor has he ever rescheduled any contact with his children. When he met Fi, he made it clear that as much as he loved her, his commitment to his children had to come first, and she agreed with this. She was able to see it wasn't a case of loving them more than he loved her. But an adult can appreciate the need to step aside and wait; children cannot.

Living with your own stepchildren and seeing them struggle with keeping contact with their own missing father can make someone see the importance of keeping contact, and to redouble their efforts in doing so with their own children. Trevor says he really feels for his stepchildren when their father lets them down, and it makes him all the more intent on keeping up the bond with his own son, Connor. Sadly, sometimes this does lead some stepfathers to ignore or neglect the task of also making a relationship with the children with whom they live, who can feel rejected and pushed out by their stepfather's visiting children. Billy was so focused on keeping the link with his own two children that he totally ignored any relationship he might have had with his new partner Adele's children.

One incentive to keep in touch with children you have lost can be to see another man having contact with your children and trying to do the best he can to father them. Adrian had parted from Gaby in anger, after a stormy marriage in which he had been violent to her and to his two children. He had sporadic contact but frequently let them down. He renewed contact after Saul moved in, mostly because he was damned if anyone else was going to have a good relationship with his children instead of him. He was quietly satisfied that his children Alison and Ian got on badly with Saul – he saw it as meaning they preferred him. Then Gaby told him that all of them were miserable and it had to stop. Alison and Ian, she told him, were unhappy and aggressive mostly because that was the pattern they had from him. She and Saul decided to seek help and the first thing they did was to stop running Adrian down and start talking to the children about the good aspects of Gaby's past with him. As the children felt better about themselves and their father, so their behaviour improved, and so too did their relationship with Saul. Adrian was so taken aback that he too calmed down and began to be friendly and positive in his relationship with Alison and Ian, and Saul and Gaby. He discovered that an improved relationship with their stepfather actually led to an improved relationship with him too.

A stepfamily can also be a **second chance** for the man who has left his own children and is now with someone else's. His partner's children can seem a heaven-sent opportunity to get it right this time, with them. Of course, this can backfire if children feel what is being demanded is that they drop their own father in favour of the new man. Ryan, for instance, was not sympathetic to his stepfather Tim's efforts to replace a man Tim saw as doing a poor job. And Ryan was right in feeling that the situation was more complicated than it seemed at first. Tim was determined not to be a stepfather like he felt his own had been. In his campaign to be a good stepfather to Ryan and Rebecca he also wanted, in effect, to go back in time and rewrite the script of his own experiences. He too had been a brother with a younger sister. In creating, as he saw it, a happy stepfamily with them, he actually hoped in the back of his mind to recreate his own family the way he might have liked it to be. This is very common and very human impulse and it seldom works. For a start, you can't change the past simply by controlling the present. And because you can't affect what has happened, you are always left feeling slightly or largely unsatisfied with what happens in the here and now. And, most important of all, the situation in front of you won't be the same as your own and the players in it are highly likely to resist your efforts to make them play to your script. As far as Ryan was concerned, he still had a dad, and he was far too angry with Tim to accept him in any way as having anything to do with him.

But stepfamilies can also be second chances for children to be back in touch with parents who might have left without appreciating them, or lost touch. Steve, Ryan and Rebecca's father, had lived with another woman after splitting up with Lynn, and had felt it right to put his efforts into looking after his new partner's own children, his stepchildren. He had been in contact with Ryan and Rebecca, but she especially had felt left out since it felt to her as if they never saw their father on their own. Having split from that relationship, he was now fully back in their lives, wanting to do right by them, and Ryan certainly greatly appreciated this contact. Rebecca, however, held off. As in many stepfamilies, she felt a variety of difficult emotions. She was angry with Steve for seeming to have preferred other children, and to an extent wanted him to feel what she had felt – rejected and left out. She also greatly feared that he wasn't to be trusted and might leave again. She misinterpreted something he had said to mean that he was planning to leave the area. A very common reaction to the fear of being abandoned is to get in first, and become the one doing the abandoning. Children have so little control and power in stepfamily situations, and often they settle on behaving badly in order to make their protest and voice their unhappiness. She fixed on refusing to see Steve again as a way to make a stand and take back some control. When she had done so – and seen him cry and heard him tell her how much he loved her and wanted to do his best – she relented. She had what she wanted – a voice – and now she could have what she really needed – both a dad and a stepdad (or as she put it a Dad and a Daddy) to care for her.

Other children who do not have contact with their own birth parents may find a new **closeness in a stepparent**. It may not be the same as having a dad of your own, but it does help and has enormous benefits. Keri has no contact with her own birth father and at first was wary of her stepfather, Noah. She was put out when her little brother Jason, who had been very young when Noah moved in, not only grew up believing he was his father, but teased her for not having a dad of her own. There was eventually an almighty blow-up in the family when Keri told him that neither did he. When the dust had settled, she and her stepfather emerged with a new and very close relationship. As he said to her, it was easy being a father to Jason, who had unreservedly accepted him – and who forgave them all for keeping it quiet that he had had a different father to begin with. But it had been more difficult staying with it to be her father, and he had done so because he loved her for herself. Keri decided it might be better to have a stepfather who stuck by you come what may, rather than a 'real' father who left.

When the going gets tough with maintaining contact between children and parents who no longer live with them, the remedy is not less but more contact. Separated parents and stepparents need to make the effort to make and keep that communication. Children and parents really do need daily contact, either face to face or by email, text and phone. If it's not possible to hear their voice or exchange emails or texts, parents might write notes or keep a diary, either to send or to keep for the next time they see the child, to reassure them the connection is always there. Above all, it really is essential for parents to stay in touch.

Things to Keep in Mind

- One in two fathers lose touch with their children within two years of a separation. Don't let it be you!

- Losing contact with a parent will always leave a hole in a child's life. How they do or do not deal with this can be at the root of life-long problems and unhappiness. Help children stay in touch, even if you want nothing to do with the other parent.

- Child/parent contact often has to be negotiated or agreed at the most stressed of times. It can be helpful to get the neutral advice and guidance of a mediator or counsellor.

- However angry you feel or difficult it is, keep parents and children in touch during and after a separation and while a new family is getting together. Trying to go back to it after a period of time is always painful, awkward and difficult.

- Ironically, losing contact with children after a separation can be the biggest incentive for someone entering a new stepfamily to 'get it right this time'. And making a good relationship with stepchildren, or having to see them struggle with keeping in touch with their own non-resident parent, is often encouragement to make good the links with your own.

- Take advantage of today's communications technology – mobiles, email, texting, etc. – to make contact easier and more frequent.

Chapter 11

Names and Identity

Names and titles are important and significant to human beings. Your own name often has particular meaning – the name of a relative, passed down to you, or one specially chosen for particular reasons by your parents. Personal names can often be shortened or otherwise played around with to make them very individual. My official name of Suzanne, for instance, is only used by a couple of school friends who have known me forever and by my mother when she is annoyed with me. My stepson and husband call me by their own nickname: Suz. Sharing a family name tells you who you are, who you belong to and with. In most cultures when women marry they take the family name of the man they join, and their shared children have that name too. This says loud and clear that these people belong together and group with each other. Titles are of consequence, too. We like having a job description that gives us some status, and to most people, being a mum or a dad is a job title they wear with pride.

This is why names can be a special cause for grief and anger in stepfamilies.

The adults in a stepfamily may feel it's important that a stepmother or stepfather be called Dad or Mum by their stepchildren. This may be particularly so if they share a house full-time, but some weekend stepparents feel it important too. Some may insist on this because they think it shows disrespect for an adult to be called by their personal name by a child. Stepmum or Stepdad wouldn't exactly feel natural, comfortable or acceptable in this society and on the whole, you can't call your stepmum 'Smummy' or your stepdad 'Sdad' and have it understood. Although that was exactly the formula Tamsin, Jonah and Connor came to with Tamsin and Jonah's stepfather Trevor, and Connor's stepmother Caitlin. Usually, the options are first names, or Mum or Dad.

The feeling behind the insistence is that somehow the name is an important indicator of how well you are doing. If you're doing a good job as a stepparent, you might expect to be rewarded – to be given a smiley face or a gold star or a badge in the shape of the name Mum or Dad. If they won't address you by that name, it feels as if they are saying they don't feel you are doing it right. They are rejecting you and telling you they don't and won't accept you as a part of their family. You're not up to scratch in the stepfamily stakes, mate.

But is this, as the advertisement says, a case of 'It does exactly what it says on the tin'? Children have two parents; the ones they are born with. One parent may have gone missing; they may have left, never to be in touch again. Or they may have died. Or be out there and sporadically in touch. Or in touch once a month and some holidays. Or around every other weekend. Or every weekend and two nights a week and on the phone every day. It doesn't matter how often they are in touch, actually. These are their parents and they cannot be replaced as parents – as Mum and Dad. Children know this, and often feel under stress and under pressure when it comes to looking at **names in their**

new family. It's bad enough losing the everyday face-to-face contact with a parent. Having their title given to someone else simply rubs salt in the wound. Having to call someone else Dad or Mum only underlines that their lives have changed and that something precious to them is missing. And that you don't seem to care or notice or realize how important this is to them.

Keeping the name Dad or Mum special and reserved for the birth parent retains a link with them when all other links may be fraying. And it takes nothing away from any new and often close relationship that children can forge between themselves and a new adult. The fact is that the thing itself isn't the same as the name. Either deciding or being told to call someone a parent doesn't mean they accept that you are a dad or mum. Stephanie, for instance, calls three people 'Dad'; her birth father, Billy, her stepfather and her grandfather. All of them are important to her and the truth is that the relationship with each and every one of them feels vulnerable. She sees Billy at weekends but doesn't seem to get on with very well, and since he and Adele broke up after Billy hit one of her sons, she has seen him less. Her grandfather has moved away and when she does ring him (he doesn't ring her) he makes excuses to cut short the conversation. And her stepfather, like Billy with Stephanie and her brother Paul, holds himself back from his stepchildren in favour of his own. So maybe she calls them all Dad as an attempt at strengthening the bonds between them, and it doesn't seem to work. Nine-year-old Josh angrily and tearfully insists he will never call his stepmother Mum, something he knows she would like. He may only see his own mother once a fortnight, but she's his mum and always will be and he loves her. In contrast, Keri calls her stepdad by his name, Noah … and adores him. He's the only Dad-like figure she has in her life and she reckons he's doing a pretty good job of it. Calling him Dad wouldn't make her accept him or love him more, just as calling him Noah doesn't make her accept or love him less.

However, you can be a really important figure to a stepchild without needing the name of Dad or Mum as a badge. Children don't see it as cheeky to call you by a personal name. Indeed, it could be argued that it does children good to know that the adults looking after them do have proper names of their own. If you're only ever Dad or Mum, it's as if that's who you are; not an individual in your own right with frailties and needs and wishes of your own, but a figurehead and institution. Mum/Dad is often seen as someone who doesn't hurt, who knows everything, who never needs sleep, time off or a life of any sort of their own beyond being Mum or Dad. Calling a stepparent by their name may not result in also calling their own parents by their name but at least it alerts them to the fact that they have one! My stepson once said he would have fiercely resisted any attempts on my part to be any sort of mother to him – which fortunately I never tried to be. And I certainly don't see that as in any way a rejection from him. I was, as he put it, a **Significant Other**. And being a good enough Significant Other is worth a lot. I might not have had a role that other people outside our own extended family understood or respected, but it worked for us. And that is the main thing and the thing you have to avoid; don't grasp at titles or names because you feel you need to, to explain yourselves to others. What you do that works between the children and other adults concerned is all that matters.

Before they, as a family, made heroic efforts and sorted out the situation between them all, Rebecca also typified one of the big debates around stepfamily names – what to do with family or surnames. When Rebecca was angry with her father Steve, and felt it really important to keep her stepfather Tim by her side, she decided she wanted to take Tim's surname as her own, and not have contact with Steve. She recognized that taking Tim's name would separate her not only from her father but also from her brother, who had no intention of losing his father's name. But since she also knew it would delight Tim, she was determined to go ahead.

It can be embarrassing, difficult and painful for children to have to negotiate the tricky question of what family name to have, especially if their mother has married the new man and changed her name. When Ben married Tina he was delighted that she took his name. He was less pleased when her younger children, a 14-year-old son and 12-year-old daughter, absolutely point blank refused to do so. And he hit the roof when he discovered Tina still used her former married name – the same name as her children – when communicating with their school or youth club. Her reasonable explanation, that she had to do so or the school or club wouldn't know who she was and which children were hers, fell on deaf ears. As far as he was concerned, her name was the same as his and that was that. He grudgingly admitted that the children had a right to keep their name, but took it as disloyalty and a personal attack on him for her to use any other, whatever the reason or circumstances.

It can be complicated in a family that might have children who have the name of the man in the house, children who have the name of a father who no longer lives with them, and maybe even children from different fathers, each with their own father's family name. You could have four children in a school who all live with each other at times, but you wouldn't know exactly where they live from their names. John and Joe Smith may share a father, Jimmy, but not a home; Jake Jones and Jenny Owen may live with Jimmy, his wife Jane and their son John but Jimmy isn't the father of either of them although they and John have the same mother. Children may be torn – this confusion and the way they may feel it singles them out could lead to their wanting to change names to be the same as the other people in their family. Equally, they may stubbornly cling to the same name as a father who no longer lives with them, to retain the link they have with him. Indeed, this is why the courts are most reluctant to let parents change children's names after separations and when new families form; if asked, they are likely to uphold a child or non-resident parent's insistence on keeping the birth name.

In fact, you don't have to go to court for a child to choose to change their name. People can actually call themselves anything they want, as long as it is not with intent to defraud or commit any offence. But if you try to change a

Personal Bill of Rights

Children have a right to their own names. Everyone in your family has rights – to feel safe, to be listened to, to say what they feel. Copy this out and stick it on the message board – it's for all of you.

1   I have the right to ask for what I want.

2   I have the right to say no to requests or demands I can't meet.

3   I have the right to express all of my feelings, positive or negative.

4   I have the right to change my mind.

5   I have the right to make mistakes and not have to be perfect.

6   I have the right to follow my own values and standards.

7   I have the right to say no to anything when I feel I am not ready, it is unsafe or it violates my own values.

8   I have the right to determine my own priorities.

9   I have the right to not to be responsible for others' behaviour, actions, feelings or problems.

10 I have the right to expect honesty from others.

11 I have the right to be angry at someone I love.

child's name for them or they do so while under 18 and the other parent objects, it can go to court and the court is likely to uphold the request to remain as it was. And so it should – you have every right to sever the link you had with the adult with whom you no longer want to share a name – partners can divorce. A parent is a parent for life, however, and children often

12 I have the right to be uniquely myself.

13 I have the right to feel scared and say 'I'm afraid.'

14 I have the right to say 'I don't know.'

15 I have the right to not give excuses or reasons for my behaviour or refusal to do something.

16 I have the right to make decisions based on my feelings.

17 I have the right to my own needs for personal space and time.

18 I have the right to be playful and frivolous.

19 I have the right to be healthier than those around me.

20 I have the right to live in a non-abusive environment.

21 I have the right to make friends and be comfortable around people.

22 I have the right to change and grow.

23 I have the right to have my needs and wants respected by others.

24 I have the right to be treated with dignity and respect.

25 I have the right to be happy.

desperately need that tie, to remain not only in contact with their parent, but with their own past, and thus themselves. If relations have really broken down, or there has been no contact for an extended period, it is something you can discuss. But it is worth considering what a change might actually mean. Can the child continue feeling connected to the people he or she lives with without a change in name? And if they did change, would that prevent for all time any question of connecting with their origins? There can be no hard and fast rules on this – what would be best for you and your child is something you need to work out. But above all it is the child's best interests, and their interests over the long term not just on the first day of school when they may be asked why they have a different name to their mother, that matters. Maybe we should all revert back to the system still in use in Iceland; children's family names are in fact the first name of their same-sex parent plus the word for 'daughter' or 'son'. So I would be Suzie Annesdottir, and my stepson Alex Victorsson. Nice!

Children often like making their own names for you. My stepson shortened my name to Suz and that became his – and his father's – special name for me. As already mentioned, Tamsin, Jonah and Connor occasionally call their steps Smum and Sdad. Rebecca has decided she had two dads – a Dad and a Daddy. If names become an issue in your family, talk it over with your children and listen with care not only to what they say, but to the feelings behind the words. Wanting to belong, to the people they live with and the people they originate with, is such a basic need and right for children. It's up to us to help them keep the links.

Things to Keep in Mind

- Names are always important and significant to people. This is why they can be a particular source of grief or anger in a stepfamily – help your child keep the name they want, and call you the name they choose.

- Keeping the names Mum or Dad for the missing parent retains a link for a child and should not take anything away from any new relationship the child may have with a stepparent.

- If a child is under 18 and you or they want to alter their name, take professional advice from both a counsellor and a solicitor.

- There is no disrespect in a child calling an adult by their first name or a pet name – in fact, it can make the whole relationship special.

- When it comes to names it should be the child's interest that is considered first – not just the adults' wish for a 'tidy' solution to the problem or one that feels right to friends or family.

- There are benefits to knowing your parent has a name of their own and isn't just a Mum or Dad all the time.

Chapter 12

Events – Festivals and Anniversaries

Festivals such as Christmas, Eid or Passover and events such as holidays and birthdays are key flashpoints in stepfamilies. It's not simply the extra arrangements that may need to be made – who sees whom, when and where – that make it so hard. Somehow, tempers run high and everyone seems to be walking on eggshells, ready at any moment to erupt. Why are such events so difficult?

Part of the problem, one which makes for annoyance among the adults, is the competing demands from separated family members. The adults with whom children live want them to be there to share whatever event or festival it is. So too do your more distant relatives – the child's grandparents and aunts and uncles on your side. Parents who no longer share a home with the children also want to see them, as do their own relatives, also the child's grandparents, aunts and uncles. If you or your ex-partner have moved away, if your or their relatives live in another part of the country, this could mean long, tedious and expensive journeys if you are to satisfy all the rival requirements. In stepfamilies, another side also intrudes – the stepparent and their relatives. A new partner's parents may also want to see them, and your partner may expect that you, their partner, and stepchildren go too. This adds another layer of demand, another set of people to be fitted in. But it can also add another layer of rivalry or antagonism, if your partner's relatives don't want to accept or acknowledge your children. Or if your side doesn't want to accept or acknowledge your new partner and any children they may bring with them.

For the children in the middle it is both more simple and vastly more complicated. Simple, in that they often have one very basic desire; for their parents to be back together and everything to be as it once was, as they remember it might have been at some 'Golden Age' event, holiday or festival before their family split up. And far more complicated, in that even children can recognize that life has moved on and new demands and needs have entered into the equation. My own stepson, when young, once said that his choice would be for all of us – his mother, father, himself and me – to share a house together. He would always have wanted his parents back together in some way so he could have daily access to them both. But he liked me; he didn't want to eliminate me from his or his father's life. Children often can't ignore the currents they know are swirling about them – they know people are upset or angry. But they also know they want to see people they still like or that are important to them.

Children want it all, and you may want what feels desirable to you. How can this make festivals so uncomfortable? All families rub each other up the wrong way at times, so what makes stepfamilies so difficult? The main reason is that while a new relationship and a new family is **a brave new beginning** for the adults involved, it's an ending for children – the final proof that their parents' marriage has died and the family into which they were born has gone. Any event that revolves around the family being all together can only highlight the fact that theirs no longer is. Festivals and holidays can be painful because they are times when we all have specific memories – the time little Johnny fell in the pool, or Dad dropped the roast chicken. Every time they come around, you can't help thinking: 'This time last year/ the last time we did this/I remember when …' and the differences really stand out. As I have already said – but it bears repeating because it is so important – a stepfamily will exist only because something dreadful has happened. A partner or the relationship itself has become a casualty for this new family to have come into being.

That means grief, anger and guilt will be floating about just waiting to land in someone's lap. But because they're poor at putting their feelings into words, kids often act sulky or uncooperative when what they're really feeling is lost and sad. Family holidays can become a focus, as the new adult believes what is needed to overcome doubts and hostility is to offer a good time. Sadly, all efforts may not only go to waste but may cause even more problems. Win them over and children may actually feel guilty at consorting with the enemy. Kids may not want to make friends with the new adult – they want their parents back, as a couple.

Children can dig their heels in about doing things the way they have always been done, and become frantic when anything is changed. This can lead to terrible rows when new family members have another system, and want, expect or demand to do it their way. Miles and Panda found they had a major row on their hands in their first Christmas as a new family, when her two children wanted stockings in bed followed by a grand free-for-all present opening under the tree while having breakfast, and his three visiting children demanded stockings over breakfast and tree presents staggered through the day; just as they'd always had it. Neither set of children would even entertain the idea of doing it the way the other family wanted it. But neither would accept the idea of their having it their way and the other doing it theirs, either. It had to be one way and one way only, and both sets demanded it must be theirs … or else! The 'or else' was major tantrums and sulks and a Christmas Day that ended in tears all round.

The reason children cling to the customs they are used to is that it is a link to the old days. Children need a sense of order and predictability at the best of times and all the more when their family is changing. Being rigid about family traditions and ways of doing things becomes a lifebelt, keeping them afloat. It's also a way of taking sides and of reinforcing boundaries and tribes – of saying, 'This is my family and you can tell so by the way we do things. As long as it's still done in this manner, I know it's my family.' When you tamper with the rules, even to replace them with something better, you risk panic because it's that signifier of safety and security you are removing. Something as innocent as the suggestion that you should sightsee first and sunbathe later on holiday, or open some presents over breakfast and some over lunch, can be met with total disgust and scorn, which actually conceals panic. 'Oh, but that's not the way we do it with our REAL Mum/Dad.' Panda tried to point out, in vain, that maybe Miles's way was better as it meant a steady trickle of treats throughout the day rather than an orgy followed by the usual boredom and sense of 'Is that all?' Her arguments fell on deaf ears because that wasn't what it was about. What the children were really saying was: 'You've sent my Dad packing, now you move strangers in on us; we protest!' The fact that the argument was over present-opening was actually irrelevant; the real argument was about the fact that they were there at all.

Zoe was devastated when her new partner Blake's two children turned up their noses at the Easter treat she had so carefully prepared. She had hidden eggs in their garden, took the kids out and told them to go and look for them.

Dealing with Stepfamily Festivals

Speak out

Admitting there's a problem, to yourself, family and friends, is the first step to getting a handle on it. People often suffer most when they have to suffer in silence. Talk it over and you discover you're neither unique nor to blame.

Listen

Ask your children's opinions and give them the opportunity to express their feelings. Allowing them to say how upset they are doesn't make it worse, it makes it better.

Accept

Accept that you all have different viewpoints and the right to differing feelings, and work to understand and make yourself understood.

Make a positive out of a negative

Kids would really like to be with both of their parents at the same time on holidays. The alternative you can offer is that they get extended playtime – going away with one family and then again with another, having the gifts from celebrations associated with a festival with one parent and then repeating it the following day with the other.

Plan

Planning doesn't destroy spontaneity, it gives you control over what may otherwise be an overwhelmingly complex situation.

Be flexible

Be prepared to find new ways of meeting at least some of everyone's needs.

Nine-year-old Sam sat on the wall kicking his heels and 11-year-old Sandra drifted around in a careless, sulky sort of way and just threw the ones she did find on to the patio. Their mother, they pointed out several times, always gave them their eggs over breakfast and didn't make them work for them. No amount of persuasion by Blake could bring them round to the idea that the hunt would be fun. Zoe had carefully planned the egg hunt because she used to love them when she was a child, but of course that was the point – nothing she liked or did was acceptable to Sam and Sandra, who saw her as the reason their father left their mother. At the back of their mind was the fact that the previous Easter, Daddy had been at home.

But adults can find that the existence of children by a previous relationship raises their hackles, too. Children from a previous relationship are the painful proof of a former love. When there is only 'weekend' or the odd weekday access, the kids may seen as an optional extra to their partner's life which can be tolerated. Once the children become part of festival and holiday planning, it becomes far more intrusive. There can be arguments over money, whether over presents or travel or living expenses when you go away. Whatever, the arguments aren't really about the cash, they're about the need to make room in your life for other people who are also loved and important to your partner. Special times in the year take on epic status, as everyone is torn in several directions at once, competing for attention. Trying to negotiate the tricky relationship between parents and new partners and all the children involved calls for the diplomatic skills of the entire UN, and it's often at **holidays and festivals** that it all falls down. It collapses because it's difficult enough trying to reconcile the different needs of any family when it comes to holidays – one of you likes sunbathing, the other adores sightseeing and everyone else wants to go to a theme park. Throw in adults or kids who are seen as interlopers and you have a whole new unstable situation.

Ex-partners may also take the opportunities presented by the pain, **demands and expectations** of a family festival to take some revenge, or make an ex with whom they are still angry dance to their tune. George has had to fight for access to his children. His ex will flout court orders and reluctantly lets him see his three children on only the one day a week the court has agreed. Since he now lives 200 hundred miles away, this means he has to make a 400-hundred mile round trip on a Sunday to see them, or stay overnight at his parents before an access visit. He was surprised to find his ex perfectly happy for him to see his children on Christmas Day and to take them to his parents' for lunch – until he realized the point, which was to make sure he couldn't have the day at home with his new partner.

Relatives can sadly take the whole situation from touchy to explosive. Grandparents who might have been merely demanding or petulant about your seeing them over the holiday period may suddenly become totally persistent and insistent that their wishes be met, or it's a family feud. At the same time, they may be partial in their behaviour. Zoe had dumped her frustration and pain about her stepchildren's initial behaviour to her on her mother. She was horrified when her mother took it so to heart that she took revenge. When Zoe and Blake took Sam and Sandra to see them over Christmas, Zoe's mum made a point of giving her blood-related grandchildren, Zoe's nephew and niece, carefully chosen and expensive presents and carelessly tossed a couple of boxes of chocolates to them. Zoe and the children had been slowly inching their way towards some sort of relationship. Being so excluded and made to feel unwelcome and different only drove them back into anger and bitterness.

Other relatives can also make things worse by being thoughtless. When Sharon and Andy had their first full Christmas together, some of the tension came about because the youngest, Rhiannon, had a mountain of presents, far more than the other three. Some of this was because she and her brother, 11-year-old Josh, had more relatives alive or in contact to give them presents than their stepsiblings, younger Josh and Sian. But there was another aspect, too. The reality is that when it comes to managing any special event or festival, you have to be fair, whatever you feel about it, and demand that other people involved be so too. **Children need to be included,** and in the same way and on the same footing, whatever their actual relationship. So Zoe's mother, whatever her feelings, should have taken the same care and shown the same generosity to Sam and Sandra as she had to her other daughter's children. But in doing so, you also need to have an awareness of the way the child sees 'fairness'. Sharon and Andy had had the good idea of spending exactly the same amount on all the children. Sadly two problems arose out of this. First, they weren't able to make the same request of other people, so some of the children got a lot more, to the envy and pain of others. But also, the things you buy and that delight younger children tend to be cheaper than those for older ones. Three-year-old Rhiannon had a mountain of presents – around twice the actual number of parcels as the others. Younger children tend not to count monetary value; they count objects. Thirteen-year-old Sian might just have been able to see that it wasn't unequal. Nine-year-old Josh felt it was, and so felt utterly rejected.

The only way out is to keep reassuring yourself that you aren't alone. You aren't a uniquely incompetent parent or step, and the kids aren't singularly wicked children. None of you are to blame – it's the situation that makes it such hard work. With a little understanding, tolerance and effort, you can deal with those family times, and make them fun again. Miles and Panda and Zoe and Blake turned their families round by acknowledging to the children their real, underlying feelings. In both families, the adults sat down with the children and said to them that they understood why family festivals were so painful.

A very helpful couple of phrases to use are 'It sounds like …' or 'It feels like …' So Miles tried, 'It feels like Christmas was hard for you because you couldn't help thinking of what it was like when Mum and Dad were together.' And Blake said 'It sounds as if you were saying Easter was awful 'cos you kept thinking of what it was like when Mum and Dad did this with you, together.'

Sometimes, we're scared of putting the fear or the grief into words in case it opens the floodgates and makes the emotion overwhelming. We almost fear that putting it into words makes it real. Nothing could be further from the truth. The feelings are there and real anyway. And having children burst into tears doesn't make it overwhelming or out of control – it helps discharge the emotion. In both families, the children cried. But having cried, they felt better. Putting it into words allowed them to examine how they felt, talk it through and eventually move on and let it go. What they had really needed was to have their feelings heard and acknowledged. The following Christmas, Miles and Panda talked it over with the kids beforehand and they came up with a compromise all of them liked – stockings in bed, some presents over breakfast and some saved for treats throughout the day. Zoe now does Easter egg hunts not only for Sam and Sandra, but for all their friends and neighbour's children too.

Things to Keep in Mind

- Plan ahead. Firmly insist that family and friends make their bid for who goes where, and apportion out your and your children's time. It may mean Christmas Day here, Boxing Day there … or the Christmas break here and Easter break there this year and next year swap. Whatever, don't get drawn into arguments or emotional blackmail.

- When you go on holiday, let each member of the family have their day to choose what to do – go to the beach, go shopping, go round ruins. Or split up, so that everyone gets their choice, and meet up at lunch or dinner to swap stories and have quality time.

- Family festivals, anniversaries and special occasions will be times when everyone in the family remembers what they have lost – people, the old family, the certainty that some things never change. Be prepared for them to be moody

- Dive below the argument – accept that it won't be the specific tradition they are arguing over or protesting against, but the fact that it symbolizes that the family is different from how it used to be.

- Children can insist on clinging to their old ways of handling events because this is an essential link with the past they have lost. Don't take it personally – it's not because they want to react against or to disobey you or a new stepparent.

- *You* may have got it sorted – don't forget other relatives and friends may need to be brought on board so they understand what might be going on and what you want and need from them.

- Firmly insist that everyone treats all the children involved fairly and equally.

- Reassure yourself that it may take time, effort and a few tears and tantrums, but if you do the work there will come at time when special occasions become a happy case of 'the way we do things in our family is …'

Chapter 13

Discipline and Acting Out

One issue that comes up a lot in stepfamilies is discipline. Stepparents worry about children not doing what they are told and defying them. Parents worry about what happens when they leave their children with their partners and whether they will be rude, aggressive or uncooperative. Stepparents often say their stepchildren only seem to show that side of themselves when their parent isn't there. New partners may despair about how stepsiblings behave when they meet, or how they get on if they live together full-time or part-time. And every adult in the equation often tears out their hair about how they will persuade or make their children 'behave well'. Again and again, the complaint is that children will say: 'You can't tell me what to do, you're not my Dad/Mum.'

Ginny, for instance, had this thrown in her face by her partner Mick's son Jon. He was rude to her and refused to listen or do anything she said, and argued constantly with her and her two children. Jon visits his father one weekend in three and a week every school holiday, and all the family dreaded him coming

– even Mick. As far as they were concerned, he was the problem, and Mick was constantly on the phone during, before or after his visits to his mother, complaining about his behaviour. Ginny and Mick were sure Jon's mother set him up to be unpleasant to Ginny and that his frequent screams of 'You can't tell me what to do – you're not my mother' came from things she had said. Jon would even say that his mother had told him he didn't have to listen to Ginny.

In many families, the only time adults really talk to kids is to tell them off. This is possibly even more acute in stepfamilies when the atmosphere is strained and critical. It is certainly often the only point of contact between parent, stepparent and non-resident parent. Frequently birth parents are called on when a child is considered to be naughty or behaving badly, not when parents want to praise or celebrate successes. Tim would call Steve when he and his stepson Ryan had been shouting at each other, to tell him 'to sort out his son'. Sometimes this is because the stepparent genuinely wants help from the birth parent. He or she may feel unable to tackle the situation themselves, or that asking the child to behave differently might be inappropriate coming from them. Sometimes, the reason for the call is to pass the parcel – not just of responsibility, but of blame. It's a way of saying 'Look what you have landed me with. If I'm having a miserable time with your child, it's your fault and I'm going to make you feel guilty about it.' Sometimes it's a genuine desire to give the birth parent a taste of what it's like with them gone. More often, it's to make the other parent the bogey person and leave the stepparent and their partner feeling it's none of their fault the child behaves like this.

Keri certainly felt at one point that her mother, Mia, and therefore her stepfather, Noah, only concentrated on the negatives. When Keri was on report at school, they would go on about her deficiencies but ignore the improvements listed. And when she tried to menion them, she got told to be quiet and not interrupt. The problem when feelings are running high and people are angry and upset is that everyone feels out of control, and therefore tends to concentrate on how to assert control. And the obvious people parents and stepparents may wish to practise control on is the children. Hence the importance of the issue of discipline. But how do children see it?

The fact is that the classic cry of 'You can't tell me what to do, you're not my Dad/Mum' is actually less a challenge or show of defiance than a cry of pain. It doesn't speak so much of insolence and disobedience as say: 'My family has broken up, I had no choice about that and I DON'T LIKE IT!' All behaviour is a way of getting what you need. Bad behaviour is actually a way of trying to show bad feelings. When we as parents or stepparents can understand what our children need and why they do what they do, we can help them help us.

Children often find it hard to understand or explain their feelings. So they tend to act them out. So-called '**bad behaviour**' is often the only way they can express their emotions and reactions. While rules and boundaries are important, it's often more effective to consider the various needs being expressed when the idea of discipline comes up. Adults wish to be seen to be in control, to be acknowledged as doing the right thing. Children on the other hand often need to have their different response to the new family at least acknowledged. If children 'defy' you, it's better to dive under the behaviour to understand what's going on than get into a head-to-head fight. Jon, for instance, had to watch his father spend far more time with Ginny's two children, 5-year-old Jonah and 3½-year-old Lindy, and their shared child 4-month-old Neo, than with him. His rudeness, defiance and refusal to listen were actually his reaction to feeling rejected and undervalued.

One thing children lose, spectacularly and thoroughly, when families break up and when they reform is control. It wasn't their choice for you to separate nor their choice for you to make a new relationship. They can feel powerless.

This can lead to their trying to gain some control and exercise some choice in their lives, often with drastic and sometimes confusing effect. Rebecca, for instance, decided to tell her father she never wanted to see him again. It wasn't really what she wanted but it satisfied one deep need – to make a point, to be heard, to take back some influence. And Vicky would dig in her heels and refuse to cooperate – it seemed the only way to have some say in her life.

Being Positive

It's easy to get into the habit of saying what you *don't* want instead of what you *do*. When we're angry with children, we tend to focus on the behaviour we're not enjoying:

'Stop that damn noise!'
'Don't play with your food.'
'Don't drag your feet.'

The problem is, all they may hear are the words describing what we don't like ... and repeat it! Instead, ask for what you *want*, not what you *don't want* – it makes a difference!

'Please play quietly.'
'Eat your tea.'
'Come and walk with me.'

When we tell children about our lack of trust or confidence in them, we give them the message that there's no point in trying; they can't manage it, and even if they did, we wouldn't notice.

'You've got a bad report from school again – playing up, as usual. You're never going to get those exams, are you?'
'Put that glass down – you'll only spill it.'
'You haven't done your chores again – I can't trust you to do anything, can I?'

But if we trust our children to be able to do things, we feed their self-belief and confidence.

'I'm confident you can pass those exams.'

When someone says 'Discipline' most of us think about punishment. It's about keeping our children in line and doing the right thing. But the original meaning of the word is 'to teach'. Discipline is something we do to help children learn. And the best way to get children to behave in ways that please us is to help them understand what they actually want and need, and to see how they can get those needs met in ways that don't upset other people.

'I'm sure you can carry a glass of water across the room without spilling.'
'I know you'll do your chores before bedtime.'

When we call a child lazy or naughty or stupid we label them. Labelling a child is like putting them into a box, stuck at being the bad boy or naughty girl for good. We don't tell them what it is they're doing that we don't like, or how to do it differently.
A better technique is to be clear about what's wrong, and what we would prefer. Instead of labelling them, *describe* their behaviour:

Instead of 'You're lazy,' say, 'You left your stuff on the floor.'
Instead of 'You're such a mess,' say. 'Your haven't combed your hair.'

Even 'good' labels set limits. Being told you're good or sweet or wonderful doesn't say what you've done to earn praise. Describing what they've done gives children a clear idea what you like. It also allows them to take a step back and view their own achievements so they can value them as well.

Try:
'You tidied up your room and left it looking so clean!'
'You walked the dog, without me having to ask!'
'I can see you've done your homework and put your clothes in the washing machine.'

It may sound odd at first. Keep it up – it pays off!

To do this we may need to get our own needs met. When concentrating on the children and how they behave, we may be ignoring the fact that we can be feeling angry, left out and rejected. We may be showing this through shouting, being depressed and not listening to them. The best way of 'disciplining' children is often to set out to help, not punish them. After all, half the time if you punish a child for acting up in a separated family, what you are actually doing is punishing them for being sad at what has happened to them and trying to let you know about it. Where's the justice in that?

It may not seem like it sometimes, but children want to please their parents and win our approval. When they feel we have understood what they need, and can understand us in turn, they have the incentive to change. If you can tell them clearly what you want and why, and respect and listen to them, you'll get a better result than simply coming down hard on them. This is why I often suggest using what I call the Mantra in talking with children.

A mantra is actually a word or sound repeated to aid concentration in meditation. The idea is to say it again and again so it trips off the tongue without your having to think about it. **My Mantra** is also called How to Say It Clearly So You Know What You Mean, the Other Person Hears You and Nobody Gets Hurt. What I suggest you do whenever you find yourself feeling fraught is to say to the other person:

'When you …

I feel …

Because …

What I would like is …

(Or,

What are we going to do about this?)'

Use it again and again and in time, it becomes like a mantra – second nature. Using the Mantra cuts down on the shouting. For a start, it takes so long to go through it that you pick and choose your fights and only say something when it matters! But more important, it helps you identify what is really going on. Sometimes it's not because of anything the child has done in the here and now but because of old angers. When you say: 'When you …' you have to identify exactly what it is the child does to make you lose your rag. That helps you and the other person see exactly what you're really objecting to. When you have to say: 'I feel …' it helps you pin down the real and precise emotion. Anger? Or fear? Or sadness? When you say: 'Because …' you really get to the point. Because the child is winding you up? Or because it reminds you of something from your own immediate or distant past? Or because you've had a bad day and the child takes the brunt of it? So is the real emotion about the child, the here and now, or something else? And 'What I would like is …' helps all of you find a solution instead of continuing to go round and round in futile conflict.

The **acting out** that so often leads to debates about discipline is because children and young people may find it hard to tell you how they feel about the changes and losses they have suffered. Instead, they are likely to show their feelings by what they do. They often believe the change or loss is somehow their fault, which can add to their confusion and make it harder for them to talk about their feelings. Children may show distress by acting younger than their age:

- wetting the bed
- throwing tantrums
- forgetting skills they've learnt
- becoming clingy and fretful
- refusing food, being picky or eating too much
- having difficulty sleeping or in waking up

Teenagers may:

- refuse to talk
- be angry
- experiment with drugs, drink, early sex

To help your children deal with life's ups and downs, one powerful and useful technique is to help them **name the emotion**. Mick finally had a breakthrough with Jon when he said to him, 'It sounds as if you're really sad I'm not with you all the time. It must feel even worse that the others are.' It took a few attempts, since Jon was cautious and wary at first. But eventually he agreed, and Mick was able to spot the need underneath – 'Maybe we need to talk more often.' This made it possible for them to move on when Mick bought Jon a mobile so he could ring and talk whenever he wanted. The three stages – Name the Emotion, Spot the Need Underneath and Use This to Move On – led to a dramatic change. Instead of having to discipline Jon, Ginny and Mick were able to transform the situation by recognizing and helping Jon voice what was really going on.

Sometimes simply recognizing and accepting the feelings and needs is enough. Other times, we may need to help our children sort out what they are going to do. Moving on may mean having to accept there is nothing that can be done to change a situation, but we can always change how we ourselves act or feel about it. First, we may need to let the first flush of emotions die down. What often blocks any advance in a stepfamily is the anger that is flying around. Vicky and Ade felt intense anger and they took it out on each other, and on her son Daniel. It stopped them creating a loving stepfamily. The problem was that both of them had anger because of experiences in their past rather than in the here and now.

Anger is a natural emotion and neither right nor wrong. It's how our anger comes out that makes it hurtful and scary, not the emotion itself. Anger is a signal that what is happening is not OK for us and we need something to change. There are other feelings underneath anger – fear, sadness, worry, frustration – and working out what these are will help us to identify what is really upsetting us and what we'd like to be different.

Feeling angry can be:
- an early warning signal that important needs aren't being met
- a push towards making some changes
- a way of helping other people understand how we feel and what we need to happen

Both adults and children in a stepfamily situation may often find themselves feeling angry, and find it difficult to deal with the strong emotions.

Feeling angry and not expressing it:
- makes us feel powerless and helpless
- means our needs don't get met
- makes us ill – depression, headaches, stomach-ache, backache
- leaks out as resentment, souring and damaging relationships
- builds up and then explodes in dirty anger

'Dirty anger' is:
- blaming, insulting, hitting or bad mouthing
- 'kicking the cat' – dumping bad feelings where they don't belong
- raking over past grievances

Feelings Jar

All of us have feelings. At times, we feel happy, sad, angry, rejected, confused and loads more. However, many of us have picked up from parents and other influences the idea that some feelings are 'bad' – not things we should be feeling. Feeling angry is often seen to be unacceptable; so is being jealous. What then happens is that when we have these feelings we feel guilty: 'I shouldn't be feeling this. I must be a bad person to feel like this.' Sometimes, we blame others: 'You make me feel angry – it's all your fault – you're the bad person!'

This isn't helpful. The truth is that all feelings are natural and having them is normal. Feelings are just feelings – we can't help them and there's no shame in having them. What we can help is what we do about them. Taking out anger on someone in an unhelpful way doesn't make us feel better, or deal with the feeling, either.

But often, we can't deal with the emotion we are feeling because we don't actually know what it really is. Children particularly can find it hard to put into words what they are actually experiencing. Next time you or someone else feels upset, use a Feelings Jar to isolate, understand and put a name to the feelings. Get an empty jam jar, write out these words – and any other words to describe feelings you can think of – mix them up and pour them out on a table. Sift through to pinpoint the word that best describes what you are feeling. You or the other person may be angry. Or, you might be feeling abandoned or worried or embarrassed. Once you know what it is, you can discuss what you might do about it. Simply acknowledging the real emotion and realizing you don't have to feel guilty for having it can help.

Abandoned	Fed Up	Nervy
Alarmed	Forgotten	On Edge
Angry	Frightened	Out of Sorts
Anxious	Fuming	P***ed Off
Bored	Glad	Panicky
Bothered	Gloomy	Peaceful
Calm	Hacked Off	Pleased
Cared For	Happy	Quiet
Cheerful	Humiliated	Rejected
Cheesed Off	Ignored	Relieved
Cold	In Despair	Resentful
Confused	In High Spirits	Sad
Content	Jealous	Warm
Cross	Jittery	Scared
Dejected	Jumpy	Sensitive
Depressed	Left Out	Shamed
Disgusted	Loved	Shown Up
Down in the Dumps	Loving	Sick and Tired
Dumped	Low	Snappy
Edgy	Miserable	Stressed
Embarrassed	Neglected	Tense
Envious	Nervous	Thrilled
Troubled	Unwanted	Uptight
Uneasy	Upset	Worried

Dirty anger does us and our children no good at all. It makes them defensive, harms our relationship with them and their self-esteem, leaves us ashamed and guilty and doesn't get the result we want. In stepfamilies, dirty anger often results in adults blaming either one particular child or several children as 'the problem', or becoming convinced that another adult is setting them up. The problem is that 'calling' or criticizing other adults only hurts children further, and often leads to them behaving even more badly. How can we express anger in a way that gets our needs met and doesn't damage those around us?

Ginny realized that she had to make some changes if she, Mick and their children were ever going to deal with one thing they couldn't and shouldn't

Positive Discipline

- Children are not born good or bad, and every child is capable of learning right from wrong. They learn how to behave by watching the adults they live with.

- When enforcing discipline focus on the child's behaviour, not them as a person. Rather than saying 'You're lazy,' say, 'I don't like it when you don't do your chores.' Labels and names like 'useless' or 'stupid' stick and can affect children's confidence if they hear them again and again.

- Explaining why you find certain behaviour unacceptable gives children the chance to learn how they can improve and develop self-discipline.

- Try to focus on good behaviour and reward it rather than on bad and punish it. Rewards can be attention, smiles, hugs, praise and thanks. When a child is attention-seeking it's usually because they both need and deserve some attention!

- Ask for cooperation rather than obedience and show that you can be cooperative in return.

change – Jon's continuing relationship with his father and so presence in their lives. She recognized that she had to start acting on the early warning signs that she was feeling angry rather than simmering until she exploded. She learnt to count to ten when Jon wound her up, and ask for a time out. When anger threatened to overwhelm her, she'd make an excuse, go up to her room and scream and punch a pillow. Then she'd take a deep breath, calm down and go back. She also started saying to Jon, 'I'm really feeling angry Jon; please stop before I lose it and shout at you.' To her surprise he responded, sometimes by laughing and saying, 'Yes, I'm angry too. I wanted you to know.' Sometimes, he would say, 'Sorry. Shall we cool off together?' By recognizing

- Children will test boundaries. Try to keep some balance and perspective about what limits they can push and which you need to stay firm on.

- Let children know how you see things and explain why you hold to a boundary.

- Children may push your limits but this is often an attempt to see how firm and secure their world is. So saying 'No' may be what they want – a lack of boundaries can be scary for children as it feels as if their world is out of control.

- As children grow older some boundaries may change. This is something you need to discuss with them. Compromising doesn't mean giving in. It may mean that you are listening and valuing their opinions and are letting your children take more responsibility for themselves.

- Treat all children fairly

- You won't get it right all the time. There's no such thing as a Perfect parent. What we want to be is Good Enough!

her own feelings and talking to him about them, Ginny found both of them could respect, understand and act on what was going on instead of blaming or fighting.

But sometimes, children in difficult stepfamily situations seem to push you too far. When children are in the grip of strong feelings they are not able to think straight or listen to reason. What they may need is to get the feelings out, safely, to calm down enough to sort out the problem.

In the face of a temper tantrum:
- Don't take it personally.
- Listen to the tune, not the words. Dive under the words to help them work out what it is they need.
- When the storm is over, acknowledge the painful and strong feelings they have been experiencing. Help them work out how they were feeling, what they needed, what they can do to express angry feelings and get what they need without hurting others.

My belief is that it's not discipline in the form of punishment or control that children need when they behave badly in a stepfamily situation. What is underneath their behaviour is often a need for attention, acceptance, appreciation, and some independence. They are often fighting to get these when they act up. We can help them by:
- talking openly about the change or loss that has lead to their being in a stepfamily
- helping them show their feelings
- sharing our own feelings with them
- telling them it's OK to feel bad, even if other people in the family are happy about the change

- telling them what's going to happen and asking their opinions
- giving them plenty of time and attention
- making sure some things don't change
- helping them keep in touch with people, places, things that matter to them
- helping them remember people, places, things that matter through photos, letters, drawings, objects
- keeping them busy doing things they enjoy
- giving them love, reassurance, support
- cutting them some slack and accepting they will act up

We need to recognize that when it comes to a stepfamily, it's the adults who choose to be there, not the children. We need to take our ability to make choices a step further – to choose to act in ways that make that choice work. And that may mean having to let go some elements – to give your children some choice and more control of their own.

Kids are far more likely to cooperate if they feel trusted and part of a team, and asked what they want rather than told what you don't. Giving them responsibility and choices neatly sidesteps disagreements. Instead of scratching your head about how to punish them, use another form of discipline – positive learning. Build a close relationship with them so that they trust you to give them attention and understanding. Notice and acknowledge their strengths and achievements. Let them make choices wherever possible. You'll soon notice the don't need to be disciplined in the form of punishment at all.

Discipline is not about doing what you are told. It's about understanding your behaviour and knowing what is acceptable and not acceptable to those around you. Discipline is a way of learning this.

Things to Keep in Mind

- Bad behaviour is usually the only way a child has of telling you about their real needs. Being naughty or defiant is a way of 'acting out' feelings which the child either doesn't understand or can't or hasn't so far been allowed to put into words. Listen, don't punish.

- Children can lose any sense of control over their own life when a family breaks up. A child who is feeling helpless may try to gain some power by taking a stand against a parent or stepparent, with the declaration: 'You can't tell me what to do, you're not my Mum/Dad!' It's not personal, so don't take it personally.

- Ideally, discipline should be about teaching not punishment. Praising often and saying Please, Thank You and Well Done gives the child an incentive to change.

- Think about how you were 'disciplined'. Was it effective? Try the 'mantra' approach as a new way of working in your new family situation.

- Children have triple-A needs in a stepfamily – ATTENTION, ACCEPTANCE, APPRECIATION. If you can negotiate these with them, most discipline problems should disappear.

● Discipline, or the apparent lack of it, can be the only thing parents really talk to children about and are often the only times exs are called on. If you want children to behave, it helps to take a more positive approach – and the same could be said of dealings with other adults.

Chapter 14

School

Most of us have two main areas in which we spend a large proportion of our lives; home and work. Sometimes we let these merge, bringing work home or socializing with people we know from work. Sometimes we keep the two apart. Children have the same; home and school. School plays a very important role in children's lives. When family change happens, their and their parent's relationship with the school can greatly help or greatly worsen their situation.

Kids may like to keep school and home separate. They tend to see an enormous difference between the two. After all, home is a place where you can eat, watch TV, get angry, speak up and even occasionally be boisterous more or less as you like. School is a place with formal rules and timetables, where you have to keep to rigid mealtimes, and may be punished for losing your temper or making a noise. Home is a place where you might expect to be hugged and accepted for what you are. School is somewhere you have to compete and excel, and have to keep a stiff upper lip. But in the process of family change, school may become a haven. The predictability of school may be a relief if home life is unsettled and unstable. It's a place that does not alter, with old friends and support when so much is shifting about them. Eamon found his school a boon, both when his parents split up when he was 12 and when his father remarried when he was 17. At both times, and in between, his teachers were understanding about his occasional moodiness and his friends stuck by him. He discovered several were in similar situations, and they could talk, compare notes and suggestions and back each other up. Eamon might have sometimes sounded off with his mother but he felt his school was a kind of refuge.

Sadly, the break-up of one family and the establishment of a new one can often mean a school transfer, as the new family moves home. This means children are uprooted even further, not only losing their old family but leaving behind friends and adults who might have helped them, removing that support network. Eleven-year-old Josh started a new school when his mum, Sharon, moved in with Andy, and he found it hard to find his feet. Children often try to hold it together at home, not wanting to put extra burdens on a parent who may be struggling with a separated family or a stepfamily. For many, school becomes the one place they can act out their anger. And for those already 'kicking off' at home, school can be another arena to display their feelings. Thirteen-year-old Ryan was fighting in his school and coming close to being excluded. Hardly surprising since Ryan had a lot of anger that wasn't being explored or heard.

It can only make things worse if misery at home is intensified by bullying or harsh treatment at school. Children often prefer not to have details of their home life made open to their school. They feel it risks having them picked out and made visible and vulnerable. This is fine when their lives in both spheres are on **an even keel**. It's often not helpful during family change. Their need for privacy, boundaries and a say in their own lives often leads them to keep quiet about trouble at school rather than bring it home to you, or risk you going to the school. The problem is that young people often do not see the connection between unhappiness at home and difficulties in school. They may not recognize that they are reacting to what is going on in their home life by being moody or failing at their studies, and that the school knowing what is going on might help.

A child may also become a school refuser in the midst of family change. Parents and the school may search desperately for reason why they might be refusing to attend, and focus on some of the usual reasons:

- bullying by other children
- treatment by teachers that shuts them out or scares them
- fear of being shown up in class, having dropped behind in studies
- the fear of punishment for not keeping up with work, or for non-attendance

The sad reality, which we may not want to accept, may be that the child is afraid of what might happen if they leave home rather than what is waiting for them at school. They may be scared that, with so much changing around them, if they turn their back to go to school they could come home to yet more surprises. It could be that they refuse school because:

- Their family is transforming, they are losing touch with people that matter to them and they don't know what else may happen next.
- A parent or sibling may be drowning their grief or uncertainty in drink or drugs and the child may be worried about what will happen while they are away.

We all want the best for our children, and parents and stepparents often hope their children will do even better than them. Chris felt school was important and he and his stepchildren often clashed over what Chris felt was their wasting of opportunities. Since children spend so much time at school, parents often feel it may be the place to turn for **advice, help and support** when children seem to be having a bad time. Fortunately, many schools do rise to that challenge. Some do not, and it may be helpful to consider what a school should, could and may not be able to offer.

The school may be the one to make a call to you, if the child is being seen as badly behaved in class. Or you might go to them, especially if the bad behaviour is coming out at home too. Parents may feel able to approach the school even when such behaviour is only experienced at home because it can feel difficult to go elsewhere. If the behaviour is happening at school as well as at home, the feeling may be 'Well, it's not all our fault – they can't do a thing with him either!' We may not want to go to the doctor and ask for a referral for specialized counselling or child behavioural support – talking with a teacher, who after all we expect to be 'an expert' in children, feels safer. Sometimes, what seems to be 'bad behaviour' in children – and something that appears to have started around the time the family broke up or the stepfamily formed – is nothing of the sort. Small children who run around screaming, grab things off the shelves when you take them shopping, draw on the walls at home or ask 'Why?' every two seconds are not naughty. They are perfectly, normally, curious. A teenager who argues back isn't being defiant or rebellious but is working through a normal stage of development – the journey towards standing on their own two feet. This would have happened anyway – it just may seem so hard to cope with at a time when so much else is happening.

A trusted teacher may help you work towards an understanding of what is going on. You, and they, will want to explore:

- what might be the cause of the behaviour
- what might help
- where support may be found

The vital questions to ask may be 'What changed around the time this behaviour started?' or 'Has this happened before – when, and what was happening then?' The answers may help you and the school to unpack what might be the trouble and to find a solution or support.

Talking to the school may be of immense help to you and your child. The point is that schools are often in the dark about what is going on in a child's life. Unless you actually tell them, how are they to know what might be affecting their pupil's feelings or behaviour? And you may be so caught up in the moment and in dealing with the fallout, you may have forgotten that what has happened may have given rise to what you're suffering, as a knock-on effect. Don was pretty sure his son Patrick's secondary school did know his mother had died when he was 10. But Don was less certain whether he had actually told them that his own mother and an aunt had both died over the Christmas holidays. Patrick was on report and in trouble over the previous two months or so, and Don realized he hadn't got round to discussing with a teacher the fact that his father-in-law and two of the family dogs had died in that time. Telling the school secretary that a child needs time off for a funeral isn't a guarantee that the vital information had been filtered to the relevant teachers, and taken on board.

Young people cannot contribute to and gain from their education unless they feel safe from ridicule and bullying, from other kids and from teachers. They need to feel safe and confident, both at home and at school. The problem is that we often feel uncomfortable when in contact with our children's school. We shy off going through those school gates or asking to speak to a teacher – especially a head or deputy head – because it feels as if we are straight back twenty or so years to being a pupil ourselves once again. If all we can remember from our school days is being small and insignificant, not being listened to, being humiliated, being powerless … it's hardly surprising we may not want to risk feeling like that again. You too can start feeling angry, defiant, defensive – not the best beginning for a reasoned, supportive and helpful chat. It may be because we are still hamstrung by the culture of silence that holds in many schools – don't tell, grass or sneak. Or it may be because we feel the teaching staff won't support, listen to or believe either us or our children. We may feel it shows us up as incompetent parents – as 'failures'. We may feel the school won't listen or will deny there is a problem – and we may be right. While many schools are making great strides in acknowledging and tackling all the issues that worry children in the middle of family change, many still are not. Some schools realize the difficulties many parents face and do their best to send out messages that welcome you in and make it clear you can speak to them. Others are less aware, so it's up to us to recognize that we may feel 12 again but be clear we are adults in control of ourselves and our own lives and be able to be in control of a situation.

Children can pick it up if you have anxieties about school, and have poor expectations from their school or schooling. **Being involved** in your child's school tells them that you value it as a place to be and a place to learn, and that learning is important. Most teachers encourage and welcome your involvement and encourage parents to take part by attending parent/teacher and open evenings. The big issue for separated parents is who goes, and who receives communications from the school.

Some schools still send notices back through children. This can be especially hard on stepfamilies on two counts. If a child goes to school from one home and travels on to another for a stay at the end of that day, a letter that is intended for the resident parent may be handed to the other – or, more often, forgotten and be lost at the bottom of a school bag. More important, one letter will be given to one parent, usually the parent the child lives with in the week. This effectively cuts off the other parent from involvement in a vital aspect of their child's life. An aspect, moreover, that both parents (and indeed perhaps the stepparent) need jointly to be involved in.

Even when schools do send vital communications by post, they often neglect to find out if parents live apart, and if so which addresses they should be sending notices to. Rebecca's school did not send her school reports to Steve as well as to Lynn, nor did Sian's send hers to her mother Kerry as well as to Andy. When Sian got a particularly good report, she had to take it to her mother some days after for her to see it, instead of it routinely arriving in the post as it had to her father Andy.

When schools do not routinely ask if parents live together, it can seem awkward and embarrassing to specify you do not. You may fear it singles out your child unfairly. But it may be far more unfair for what might be understandable difficulties not to be understood if the school doesn't know the circumstances. Sean was usually on the ball about having his games kit or the proper books with him. Every so often, he turned up at school without. His teachers were lenient and understanding – it's hard to keep track when you may arrive to school from one home, and go home to another. When Donna dropped her 9-year-old son Dwight off for an after-school club she was later horrified to hear it had been cancelled. She rushed to the school to find it closed, and then home to see if he had managed to find his way there. She was relieved to get a call on her mobile from her ex. The teacher in charge knew Dwight had two homes and in spite of Dwight's obvious embarrassment and caginess had managed to find Dwight's father who came to get him. If the teacher hadn't known the situation, he might have given in to Dwight's insistence that it was all right to walk home – a mile, to an empty house as his mother was at work.

Children benefit from having both their parents show an interest in their schooling, even when you do not live together. It's really vital that both parents receive notice of parent/teacher meetings and that you have some agreement between you, and the school, about how you are going to manage this. Not only can you ask the school to make sure information is sent to more than one address. You can also ask for special help if work or family commitments make it difficult for both of you to attend parent/teacher meetings. Instead of both parents going to the parent/teacher meetings together, you could ask for one of you to have a one-to-one with members of staff at other times. I once attended an open night at my stepson's primary school. Whist his parents talked to his teachers, he showed me round and we bumped into the headteacher, who cheerfully asked if I was his mother. Oh no, he said. I was his father's 'flatmate'. He was most amused to watch the head struggle with that one. Some stepfamilies may feel it appropriate for stepparents to talk to teachers, too – if you are intimately involved in the day-to-day life of the child and their schooling, it does seem fair. But parent's and the child's feelings need to be taken into account.

You may have a fight on your hands with the child when you want to tell the school what is going on. *You* may accept that it helps to tell them so they can understand the circumstances surrounding a child's behaviour. *Children*, however, may say they don't want to let their school know about family change or problems. It's often tempting to give way on this. Young people may feel unwilling to let you know if they are having problems in school. They may feel you have too much on your plate already, or can't help them anyway, or feel school and home are two separate worlds and should be kept apart. I'm all for respecting a child's choice and wishes, but sometimes we have to take

School Check

Ask them:

- How do you take children's different family circumstances into account? Do pupil records show if parents live together or if children live with adults who are not related to them? Do they make a note if children have more than one address they stay at regularly? Are the records you keep on children kept up to date and are they changed if the child's circumstances change? Do you make sure all members of staff who deal with a child know about what is happening to them?

- What do you do about parents living at separate addresses? Do you keep the parent who doesn't live day-to-day with the children informed about reports, school events and trips? Do letters sent home assume both parents live there?

- Does the school accept that family change is normal? What are teacher's attitudes? What do you teach about family lives? How might a child's family circumstance come up in the classroom? Do the teachers and the learning materials indicate that families come in all shapes and sizes?

- How do you know if pupils are having difficulties in their family lives? How do you think such difficulties may affect pupils, parents and the school? If children have problems or get into trouble, are their family circumstances or how they may be feeling about this taken into account?

- How do you help children who are new to the area? How do you deal with a child who arrives during the school year?

- Can you do more to support pupils with family problems? Does the school have a formal policy to offer support, or does it only happen if a particular member of staff takes a lead?

- What sort of extra, outside help can you recommend? How good are your links with outside help?

responsibility for stepping in. The fact is that schools really do need to know what is going on, to make sense of what our children do or say or feel while in their charge.

It's important to recognize you're not alone in struggling with a lack of confidence in speaking to teachers. It's a common difficulty and will be shared by many other parents of children at this school. It might help you, and other parents, to take a checklist to the next meeting you have with the school. You can use this both to check on what your child's school is doing; to inform them of your situation; and to ask for changes if they don't come up to scratch.

Things to Keep in Mind

- Just as most adults have a life which is divided between home and work, so children have a life that is divided between home and school. School is nearly half of a child's life and its significance and potential influence should be recognized in all our dealings with our children.

- Most children will try to keep home and school separate. To someone in a stepfamily, school may either be a place where their troubles are multiplied or a haven and an escape from any confusion or unhappiness at home.

- Stepchildren may feel safe to act out their feelings in school in a way they cannot do at home. Bad behaviour at school is often a symptom of upset at home and needs to be dealt with in this light.

- Teachers are not mind-readers. You should always tell them immediately of any events in a child's life that might be behind what may otherwise be labelled 'bad behaviour'.

- Make sure the school is aware of a child's situation and arranges to send copies of reports and notes to both parents.

- The best way of ensuring a child has a successful school life is for you to take as active an interest as possible. Keep in the loop by talking over their day with the child, or consider being part of the school process itself as a member of a parent/teacher group or a school governor.

Chapter 15

Image

Most of us only hear about stepfamilies through stories – especially fairy stories – before we actually find ourselves in one. From Cinderella's stepmother and the Ugly Stepsisters, through Sleeping Beauty's Wicked Stepmother, to the Stepfather in a fairly recent horror movie, stepfamilies, stepfathers and stepmothers have a terrible press. There is a wealth of bad association with the words; stepmothers are always wicked, stepfathers always evil or mad, and stepbrothers and sisters scheming and selfish. It's hardly surprising therefore that children may approach the situation feeling worried and nervous. Petra (15) and David (12) admit that all their school-friends warned them how awful it would be with a Wicked Stepmother in the house, and they've found it hard to see past the image. Keri, on the other hand, finds that no matter how many times she reminds her friends Noah is her stepfather, they insist on referring to him as 'your dad'. Why? Probably because they think he's really cool, and Keri loves him. If he's cool and she likes him, he can't be a stepdad, can he? Because stepdads are nasty. Everyone knows that.

The image that stepfamilies have can prove a real stumbling block as you and your family try to put together your new living arrangements. For a start, it may be hard for anyone to actually accept that what you are in IS a stepfamily. The parenting charity Parentline Plus say that many calls to their helpline are from stepfamilies who clearly don't call themselves or see themselves as anything of the kind. On one hand, you may say this is a healthy state of affairs, in that such families see themselves as simply that – a family. But on the other hand, if you don't define yourself as a stepfamily you may not be able to recognize that some of the problems you may be having are entirely to do with that. In other words, not because someone is being nasty or foolish or selfish, but because the situation is fraught and tricky and can give rise to difficulties. But if you feel that stepfamilies are bad things you wouldn't want to be in, you may decline the name. The fear is a superstitious one; accept the name and the problems that go with it will fall about our heads. Refuse the name, and we'll be safe – it won't happen. Alas, refusing to take on the title doesn't mean you suddenly and magically aren't in the situation.

Stepfamilies really suffer from the fact that the image of what a family should be, and what a stepfamily is supposed to be, comes between what they might be able to build and what they may be struggling with. Families are believed to be made up of people who love each other, and this love proceeds naturally from the fact that they are related. It is feared that a stepfamily is a place where unrelated people are thrown together and there will be rivalry, jealousy and separation at the heart of it. We tend to approach the whole subject of families with a whole lot of 'oughts', 'shoulds' and 'must bes': I ought to love this child, this child should listen to me, I must be the perfect parent. Parents suffer enough under this burden of what they think they ought to do and be – stepparents may suffer even more.

Not wanting to put yourself in the frame of 'Stepfamily' often means that if the going is hard, we start imagining that's because someone is making it hard. It's easy to start blaming the ex, the new partner or the children involved. If there are arguments, we may want to feel that someone is to blame, not ourselves, and who else better to blame than someone who does not reflect on us – another person's child, another person's partner, someone we no longer live with. It's a lot easier to dump the whole difficult, painful mess on to someone else's lap than to have to explore, understand and maybe accept responsibility for a complex situation that is partly our task to address.

Coming into a stepfamily, we may come face to face with two conflicting beliefs. One is that you can't love children who aren't your own. The other is that an adult has to feel love for a child they look after. Can you love someone who is not your child/not your parent? Yes … and no. Yes, you can come to love a child or parent almost as much as you might a child or parent of your own, given time and patience and living together. After all, you love a partner even though they are not blood-related so being related is not necessarily the point. But it may need time and patience and the experience of living together, and this is what makes some people anxious. Because your own relationship with a parent or child seems to suggest the parent/child bond is gut-deep, instant and powerful, you fear that if it doesn't happen at once and in the same way, it may not happen at all. You start fearing that the fact you can't summon up any positive emotion for this stranger may mean there is something wrong with you. Since you don't want there to be anything wrong with you, you start casting around for reasons why it isn't happening. Aha, you cry, it must be because the person in question isn't lovable. It's because of something in them that I can't summon the feelings – they must be bad, heartless, not worthy of my love. It's their fault, not mine!

And why should you feel instant love for them? Look at the way the animal kingdom manages these things. Lions who take over a pride kill the cubs of the previous male. Sheep won't foster orphan lambs unless shepherds make strenuous efforts to fool them into thinking it's their own lambs they are suckling. In the natural world, animals on the whole do not foster and do not stepparent; they look after their own and only their own. We are different – we have the capacity to think and to overcome our instincts. But it's necessary to at least recognize that instinct does go against us. If we're to overcome the instinct to push the stranger bird out of the nest, we first at least need to understand and recognize and accept the impulse is there.

One way to tackle the **myths and bad press** is to at least acknowledge it. When Mina met Zach's's two children, Ethan and Kim, she cheerfully introduced herself as the Wicked Stepmother. The first Christmas they shared, she took her daughter Amber, Kim and Ethan to see the pantomime *Sleeping Beauty*, and gleefully told them she had a special mirror in her bedroom, too. By making a joke of it, she took the sting out of any tales the children had heard. Kim demanded an apple as soon as they got home and she and Amber rushed off to play with it, with Amber as the Wicked Queen, herself as Sleeping Beauty and Ethan acting as the prince. Connor sends birthday and Christmas cards to Caitlin addressed to My WSM – My Wicked StepMother.

Above all, confronting the stepfamily and family myths helps you think about what might be different and good about your particular set-up. It is different to the traditional family – but traditional families aren't always what they are cracked up to be. In the Good Enough family, you would always have a parent ready to listen and be there for you. Sometimes, in 'normal' families this isn't so. Second-time families, in being a second chance for adults in their relationship, also can be a second chance for adults to be the parents they might have wanted to be. Having a father, a mother and one or two

Significant Others often means a child always does have an adult to turn to, even when other adults have their hands full or their minds on other things. It may mean you have siblings when otherwise you might not have, or siblings older or younger when otherwise you might not. It also sometimes helps to have adults who are close enough and involved enough to care deeply for you, but by not being a relative, capable of being objective. And sometimes it's good to have a close and caring adult to talk to about the sadness that another adult causes you.

Being a parent is a hard job. The pressure we often put on ourselves to do it perfectly can make it worse. If we want to help our children feel good about themselves, start with yourself. You, too, need to relax and feel good about yourself. 'I ought to …', 'I must …', 'I should …' are all messages that make life stressful. And while stress can be helpful and get us going, it can also exhaust and put us on a knife edge, ready to blow.

- Go easy on yourself. You don't need to be perfect – there is no such animal as a perfect parent. Being Good Enough is the aim.
- Do some things just for yourself – some exercise, some relaxation some time alone. You'll return to being a parent refreshed.
- Do the things you have to, not the things you feel you 'ought' to, and reserve some time for the things you want to do, too. If you can make time for the important things you can make time for yourself. You are, after all, important.
- You feel stressed when you feel out of control. So take control of the things you can and you'll feel better.
- Act, don't react. If you're feeling tired, upset, stressed, the chances are it's because you need something. Get your needs met and you will regain control.

Self-esteem is knowing you matter. It means you feel worthwhile and confident, able to deal with problems and manage your life. Someone with self-esteem knows they are as important as anyone else – but no more.

We build self esteem in others, and foster it in ourselves, by:

- valuing and accepting – ourselves and other people
- respecting, caring for, loving those close to us
- listening to others and asking them to hear us
- taking time, with other people and ourselves

Children learn to value themselves if we value them. If you've been unlucky enough to have lost out in your own childhood, you can make up the loss yourself. Self-esteem goes up when our feelings are acknowledged and our needs are met – both by ourselves and by other people. Value yourself and other people will too.

Things to Keep in Mind

- The conventional image and attitudes towards stepfamilies can be a major stumbling-block as you try to arrange your own.

- Refusing to recognize yourself, or just not seeing yourself, as a stepfamily can mean you do not appreciate that some of your problems may be nobody's fault but entirely due to your being in that situation.

- You can love someone else's child and they can love you, if you put time, patience and effort into it. But don't beat yourself up if it doesn't happen at once, and don't have unrealistic expectations of yourself, or of the child.

- One way to tackle the myths and 'bad press' about stepfamilies is to acknowledge the state openly at all times and with everyone – to even make a joke about it.

- Confronting the myths directly and honestly can make you think about and recognize what might be different and good about your new family arrangements.

- Parents can have a pretty hard time of things – stepparents can have it even harder. Don't add to the inbuilt burdens by getting caught up in the 'I ought, should, or must' beliefs you may have picked up from the image and myth makers.

Chapter 16

Final Word

Can you manage to bring your stepfamily together on your own? Of course you can. It takes some time, effort and patience. It takes the honesty to consider how the unfinished business and baggage from the past affects the future and the strength to look at these issues and deal with them. It takes respect – of adults for children, children for adults and adults for each other. You may need to let go of the myth that your ex is a demon out to get you, or that one particular child is the 'baddy' at the root of all your problems. But you can do it, and I hope you do.

You might like to use the strategies, games and ideas I've outlined in this book. You may like to ask for help. You could contact organizations such as Parentline Plus on their helpline or through their website. You could see a mediator from your local mediation service or counsellors – go to Relate or find one through your own family doctor or via the British Association for Counselling and Psychotherapy. You'll find out how to contact all these and more in the Links section. You may also get in touch with self-help groups in your area or on the internet, but take one warning on that. It can be a great relief to be in touch with other people going through the same difficulties as you. It can reassure you to realize you're not the only one, and you can share good ideas on making changes. But you can also find yourself getting stuck in a blame culture that insists exes are evil and stepchildren unreasonable. Join up with others in the same situation, by all means. But ask them, and yourselves, to **find solutions** rather than simply hash over the problems.

As an example of how it can be done, look at the story of Lorraine and her new partner Ed, his 10-year-old son Gerry, her 14- and 12-year-old daughters Kris and Edi, her ex, Des, and his ex, Eliza. Not forgetting their new baby, PJ. Lorraine and Ed had been together for three years, married for two.

Gerry stays every other weekend and one or two nights a week. Since he lives quite some distance away, Kris and Edi see their own father one weekend in three and don't see him midweek. This means that on a six-week cycle, Lorraine and Ed have two weekends when they have all three, two weekends with Kris and Edi, one weekend when they have Gerry on his own and one weekend when all three children are with their other parent and they only have the baby.

Lorraine and Ed asked for help because, they said, Kris and Edi did not respect or get along with him. They'd cheek him and tell him he couldn't tell them what to do as he wasn't their dad. There would be shouting matches and slamming doors and a terrible atmosphere in which PJ screamed for hours at a time. It got worse on the weekends that Gerry came to stay. Gerry, Kris and Edi argued a lot at first, particularly as the girls had to share a room so Gerry could have somewhere to stay. The family moved to a four-bedroom house, but the fights between them only improved when PJ came along. At first all three hated PJ, but after a time they all got used to playing with him and seemed to enjoy him. Except that all three began being rude to Lorraine as well as to Ed.

Kris and Edi said they liked Ed and were pleased that their mum had someone to look after her, but they complained that he took more notice of Gerry than them, and that Gerry got away with murder when he came to stay. They were clearly hurt that even Lorraine said the house was quieter and nicer on the one weekend in six that Gerry was with them on his own.

Both Lorraine and Ed also had issues with the exes. Ed said Eliza deliberately filled Gerry up with stories about how happy they were, so Gerry would constantly pine after the way his family had been and want it back. He covered the wall of the room he had at Lorraine and Ed's with photos of himself, his mother and Ed when they'd all been together, and Ed knew his room at home was the same. Kris and Edi also had photos of both their parents and themselves on their bedroom walls, but Ed refused to have any family portraits apart from the new family in their sitting-room. Lorraine hated it when Kris and Edi went to visit their father – they'd come back surly and miserable and she was on the point of stopping it all together. After all, she said, they clearly didn't enjoy it and he wouldn't miss them as he never bothered to ring in between weekends. He had been out of contact for a few years and had only started seeing the girls again after Lorraine and Ed got married. Lorraine thought he only did it to get at her since his new girlfriend argued with the girls and obviously didn't want them around.

They had a particularly difficult Christmas the first year they were together. Lorraine's parents, Izzie and Peter, expected the whole family to come to them, as usual. Ed wanted to see Gerry and arranged to go over to him in the morning – Izzie and Peter took this as a personal insult. Ed's parents Sheila and Eric also expected to see Ed and Gerry and were hurt that this was put off until Boxing Day. When Ed turned up with Lorraine, Kris and Edi as well as Gerry it obviously caught them off guard – they had a pile of presents for Gerry and none for Kris and Edi. Gerry's other grandparents, Pat and Frank, were utterly insistent that they only wanted to see Gerry, and Kris and Edi's other grandparents, Sandy and Cynthia, simply refused to be involved at all – no presents, no cards.

The second Christmas, Ed and Lorraine tried to protect the children from hurt and rejection by arranging a Christmas all on their own. But presents on Christmas morning caused even more quarrels than the previous year. Gerry wanted presents the way he was used to having them – all to be opened one by one round the tree with breakfast on their laps. Kris and Edi wanted them the way they were used to – stockings left on beds to be discovered when they woke up, a few parcels before breakfast then breakfast round the table, then parcel-opening staged throughout the day before and after lunch and over tea. Izzie and Peter had sent presents for everyone, and Sheila and Eric had made some attempt, though Gerry's presents were obviously better than Kris and Edi's. But Kris and Edi's other grandparents had sent nothing. So Gerry had more far presents than anyone, and the day blew up into arguments, tears and tantrums.

When Ed and Lorraine asked for help, they said they really wanted theirs to be a proper family, with everyone getting on. The kids said the same – they hated the way their family was so unlike their friends'; huge rows, bitter arguments and no one really happy.

The difficulty when families know there is something wrong is what they might be prepared to do to get it right. You can turn around even the most argument-ridden family if all of you – or most of you – are prepared to do what families such as Tim's and Lynn's and Tracie's and Chris's did in the TV series. That is, take **a long, hard and honest look** at what is happening; be prepared to understand and take on board the feelings underneath the behaviour; and do some hard work to make changes.

Ed and Lorraine took a deep breath and spent some time talking over their problems. What came out was that both of them had baggage from the distant past holding them back. Ed's father was a bit of a disciplinarian. Ed had the idea from him that being a good father meant making people toe the line. Virtually the first thing he'd do when he came in from work in the evening was quiz the girls about their schoolwork, and if they hadn't got top marks, he'd lecture them. When Ed and the girls argued, Lorraine would jump in and take over, telling all of them off. From her mum she had the idea that a mother's role was to keep the peace and smooth everything over.

Lorraine insisted the girls did chores around the house, but she wasn't very good at keeping them to it. Ed felt Gerry was too young to do chores. Since Gerry didn't do chores at home, he said his mum would have something to say if he had to work when he came to stay. Gerry said he really liked coming to stay and he, Keri and Edi did get on well now, but sometimes he felt a bit left out.

Lorraine, Ed, Kris, Edi and Gerry played the hats game – writing out slips of paper with all the labels they could think of, such as Mummy's Little Helper, Black Sheep, Policeperson, Angel, Little Prince, Little Princess, Bad Girl, Bad Boy, Sergeant Major and others. They all agreed that Ed was the Sergeant Major, Lorraine the Policeperson, Kris the Bad Girl and Edi the girl in the veil who kept her head down. They also said Gerry was Ed's Little Prince, but they thought he was the male equivalent of a Little Madam.

Lorraine was shocked that everyone thought she was on their case all the time, and then realized it was actually more of a burden to her than them. She hated always having to feel she needed to watch her daughters and Ed and make sure they got on, but it was quite a step for her to recognize that her constantly smoothing things over meant they never had a chance to sort it out themselves. She was determined to leave them to it in future – but the first thing that had to happen was that Ed had to recognize that his manner was counter-productive. When Ed started lecturing, Kris and Edi switched off. Ed and Kris did an eggtimer exercise, and in it Kris told him she really liked it when he said nice things to her. She described what it felt like when he praised her for scoring a goal in her school football game, and how it spurred her on to try out for a club team. Ed was stunned – he couldn't even remember telling her 'Well done', and he realized that might be because he very seldom did so. Ed decided to ban himself from criticizing. From then on, he said he'd praise when the girls did well and ignore it when they did badly. No, they said – it'd be OK if he noticed when they didn't do well but they'd prefer if he offered to help, not turn it into a rant.

Ed started doing a chill-out session when he came home. Instead of going straight into the kitchen and, still in his work clothes launching into quizzing the girls, he went upstairs, washed and changed and lay down for five minutes with a favourite music track on his headphones. Then he came down to share a meal with everyone. Round the table, everyone – including parents – had to say:

- one thing they wanted to share with the others about their day
- one thing they were pleased they had done that day a school or work
- one thing they think they could have done better

Instead of a time for the sergeant major to cross-examine them, the meal became a fun time of the day with everyone giving an account of themselves, and laughing and enjoying it.

When Edi did an eggtimer with Ed, she said she wanted him to treat Gerry the same as them – or them the same as Gerry. She said she wasn't asking him to feel the same about them, just be the same to them. One way the girls particularly wanted equality was over chores. Ed realized he had to look at this. He saw that he didn't want Gerry to do chores because he wanted him to enjoy coming to see him – to want to come. And he feared that if he laid down too many rules, Gerry might not want to come. Lorraine helped Ed see how silly this was – Gerry wanted to see his Dad, there was no question of that. So they redid the chore chart.

All of them sat down and over a sometimes heated discussion came up with a fairer system. It meant all five of them did something round the house – Gerry was asked to lay the table and wash up when he came to stay. And instead of linking pocket money to chores – which often meant Kris got hardly any – Ed agreed to pay standard pocket money with extras for such things as cleaning the car, washing windows and mowing the lawn. Privately, he was certain it would mean Kris and Edi would be even worse at forgetting their chores. After the discussion, which 'sold' the idea of chores to Gerry on the explanation that it made him a full member of the house, he was delighted to find the girls took the idea on board too. They kept to the system and didn't miss a beat.

Ed rang his ex, Eliza, and explained what he was doing. He didn't argue – he just said, calmly, that he perfectly understood she might have a different system in her home but in his and Lorraine's, kids did their share and so would Gerry. To his amazement, she was friendly and agreed. In fact, she said she might do the same herself in future, now Ed was taking on the hard work of getting Gerry broken in to housework.

Lorraine and Ed also realized that hand in hand with doing chores, they needed to look at some rules. They saw the point of having a system of House Rules, to bypass the 'You can't tell me what to do, you're not my dad/mum' syndrome. They went back to the table – but this time, started off by setting up a Family Round Table agreement. They found an object they all agreed was the discussion 'baton' – an old opium pipe Ed's grandfather had brought back from Burma and which normally sat on the mantelpiece. The rule was that anyone with the pipe had the floor and no one could interrupt. Kris led the discussion and kept a list as the family ideas-stormed the rules they wanted. This time, the discussion was lively but not heated. They came up with a list of rules all of them agreed to, and they signed a contract to say so. And the next time Ed told Gerry not to shout, and he opened his mouth to give cheek, Kris calmly pointed at the rules on the wall in the kitchen and said, 'Uh-huh. You signed, Gerry!' Gerry zipped his lip, and said sorry.

It also meant Lorraine felt far better about about giving up her policeperson's role. The children now accept the idea that Ed, or any of them, had as much right to pull everyone up on bad behaviour. And Lorraine and Ed could start letting the kids sort out their own disagreements. They realized they shouldn't feel guilty if their children disagreed. You can't take responsibility for how children get on and some siblings will always fight. But you can limit the hurt and help them find ways of solving their own disputes. Lorraine and Ed did this by getting into the habit of acknowledging their feelings. The next time Kris and Edi had a spat, Ed said 'It looks like you are both really angry with each other.' He tried the trick of listening to and reflecting back each person's feelings and needs out loud: 'Kris, you want to watch TV, and Edi, you want quiet to do your homework' He found that explaining the difficulty with respect really helped. 'It's hard when you both want things that clash, isn't it?' Kris and Edi stared at him, then nodded. 'Fine,' said Ed, 'I trust you to sort it out by yourselves. I believe you can sort this out in a way that works for both of you.' And then he left them to it. 'You can come and tell me what you've decided if you like.' Ten minutes later, both girls came to tell him they had decided Edi would go into the kitchen, Kris would turn the sound down and Edi would make them both a drink when she was finished. Sorted – and without a screaming row or punishment from Ed.

Ed and Lorraine realized their main role when kids rowed with each other should be to underline the message that everyone is valued, respected, loved and listened to in your family. The only time you might intervene is when:

- kids are hurting each other
- a child's self-esteem is being affected
- what's happening is dangerous – such as fighting while you are driving
- when they are smashing up the house

At such times you can stop what is going on with a calm, clear but firm voice saying, 'I'm frightened someone will get hurt. Stop now. I can see you're angry but say it with words.' You can take action by removing a child or the thing they are arguing over and asking for time out. When everyone is calm, you can listen separately to each child, acknowledge the feelings and needs that lead to conflict and make clear to both children that you would like them to find a solution you can all live with. Ed and Lorraine tried this – they stopped shouting when the kids were, and calmed it down. To their amazement, the violent rows they had all got used to died out. When the kids got angry, they now:

- said it in words not by hitting, shouting, screaming
- or they wrote it down
- or they drew a picture to show their feelings
- or they worked off steam by running, playing or kicking a ball

They also put up a message board. They already stuck school certificates and notes on the fridge door, but realized a board would be even better. Everyone was encouraged to put stuff up – Gerry put copies up of his swimming certificates, and notes to his dad, stepsisters and Lorraine about what he wanted to do when he next came to stay. All of them used the board to stick up things they were pleased about or wanted other people to see. Kris really, really wanted to go on an aerial obstacle course she had read about but it would cost the family almost £70 – she was reluctant to say anything unless she got shouted down. So she got hold of the leaflet and left it on the board. One by one, everyone looked through it and thought 'That sounds fun!' Ed finally said he'd take the whole family on it if they all did extra chores for free for a month and it was the half-term treat. They all voted it was a grand idea.

Ed and Lorraine also realized it wasn't 'bad' for the other children to have felt jealous and angry about the arrival of PJ. In fact, he had brought them together – but Kris and Edi still felt slightly rejected by Lorraine having another baby. It felt as if she had said, 'You're now surplus to requirements – I've got a new one!' and that was why they had taken to cheeking her. So she made a point of dropping PJ off at his grandparents every Saturday morning so the three 'girls' could go shopping together – some girly time that made a great difference.

After the success of Ed talking to Eliza about chores, Lorraine decided it was about time she put some of the ideas that seemed to be working so well in the family to work on her and her ex, Des's, relationship. She wrote to him, saying she was sad that after the fun and good times they once had, and the two delightful children they had produced, all they seemed to do now was be bitter and angry. She said she now understood that the reason Kris and Edi found the weekends with him were so hard was because they loved him and missed him, as they had every right to do. They came back churned up not because he had done anything to sadden them or make things hard for her but because they were distressed at leaving him. She asked if it might be possible for them to see him more often – one weekend in two perhaps. If not, would it be possible for him to agree some contribution to their mobile phone bills so they could ring him whenever they wished. She waited two weeks for a reply and when it came it knocked her socks off. Des rang to ask if he could come and collect the kids for their weekend – he usually asked Lorraine to drive them or put them on a train. He came in, nodded cordially at Ed and sat down to talk over what she had said. He missed them too, and it made him miserable and angry that when they came, the weekend always seemed to end in arguments. He said it had never occurred to him that the reason they did this as because they were gloomy at leaving – he thought they got fed up with him, and this was why his girlfriend had a go at them. As soon as it was explained, he saw the point. Yes, he'd love to see them more often. Yes, he thought it was a great idea to talk to them more often. Yes, he and Lorraine should stop bickering and start co-parenting.

Ed and Lorraine stopped feeling angry that their children had another parent and loved them too. They put some pictures of their previous family – Ed with Eliza and Gerry, Kris and Edi with Des and Lorraine – in the living-room. After all, their past was theirs and should be a part of the present family too. It felt odd at first but they got used to it – and the kids loved it. And it was noticeable that with a better atmosphere, PJ stopped screaming. And Ed and Lorraine decided that next Christmas they would be proactive. They would contact all the grandparents – Des's parents too – and say the kids wanted to see them so could they agree some sort of rota, either over the break or this year one place, the next another. And – for them all to realise – there were three children in this family so please give equal presents or none at all.

Ed's and Lorraine's family is a very normal one. The couple bicker occasionally. They all disagree and argue. But they now resolve their arguments, using the techniques you can use, too, by respecting each other, listening to each other, finding the middle ground and offering some give and take.

If it all sounds very idyllic and you think, 'But that wouldn't work in my family!' why not give it a go? Look at it this way – what have you got to lose? What are your options? You can:

- stay as you are
- opt out and go under
- do some work and make it better

Many families feel so stuck in hopelessness and helplessness that they stay as they are. We sometimes feel it's best not meddling, in case things will get worse if you do. But doing nothing IS doing something. It's making the choice not to act. And if you stay like that, you will go on feeling terrible, being sad, watching yourself and your family suffer. In some cases, the next choice then gets thrust upon you – either the adults give up and go their separate ways, or children grow up and leave home. But they don't leave home with a feelings of excitement and anticipation, happy to come back at will and tell you about their adventures – they leave in anger, sadness and bitterness and can't wait to turn their back on you.

In contrast, you can ACT. You can look at your unfinished business and finish it. You can dig out all that baggage, and sort it. Yes, it may hurt. Yes, it may feel as if you're opening a can of worms and for a time it feels worse than before. But the fact is that the worms are seething about ready to ooze out anyway. Sit on them, and they will emerge at some point, and often when you least expect it or are least able to deal with them. Make the choice and take control and you have the upper hand. If you watched the BBC TV series you will have seen what happened in quite a few families who felt they were at rock bottom and couldn't do anything ... and found they could. And that the happy stepfamily they thought was far beyond them was actually in their grasp. Of course they had to work for it, and they did. And what results they got!

Do the work on your own, and you may be amazed at far you can get. Do it with a counsellor, and you can do it in safety with guidance and support. The key to remember about going for professional help, whether mediation or counselling, is that you remain in control. No one tells you what to do. They help you make up your own minds and opt for decisions that are right for you and that you can manage. Which is right for you – a counsellor or mediator?

Both could be useful. A mediator helps you and other members of your family settle disputes – they support you in deciding matters such as contact arrangements and finance. A counsellor will help you delve a bit deeper and understand why difficulties are happening and guide you in making changes to stop it continuing.

Above all, realize that YOU can all make a difference and make some changes. All it takes is the will to do it. The ideas are here. The proof is in the many families I have heard from and heard of, and the ones you see in the *Stepfamilies* series, who have made the changes.

Give it a go! Good luck!

Links

PARENTLINE PLUS

520 Highgate Studios

53-79 Highgate Road

Kentish Town

London NW5 1TL

Helpline 0808 800 2222

(24-hour, everyday, freephone)

www.parentlineplus.org.uk

Has a 24-hour-a-day, everyday, helpline for anyone with any concerns who is parenting children or stepchildren, has a website with a wide range of information and publications to send off for or download and offers parenting courses all over the country.

CRUSE BEREAVEMENT CARE

Cruse House

126 Sheen Road

Richmond

Surrey

TW9 1UR

Tel: 0208 939 9530 (office)

Opening Times: (Mon-Fri, 9.30am-5pm)

E-mail: info@crusebereavementcare.org.uk

Tel: 0845 758 5565

(helpline number for Wales)

0870 167 1677

(helpline number for the rest of the UK)

Cruse aims to give a nationwide service of the highest standard of emotional support, counselling and information to anyone bereaved, regardless of age, race or belief. Cruse also offers training, support, information and publications to those working to care for bereaved people. Cruse delivers its service through 180 branches and nearly 7000 volunteers in the community nationwide. Some branches also run friendship and social groups and drop-in centres. To contact your local branch please call the Head Office number.

THE COMPASSIONATE FRIENDS

53 North Street

Bristol

BS3 1EN

www.tcf.org.uk

E-mail: info@tcf.org.uk

Tel: 0117 9539639 (helpline)

A national self-help organization of bereaved parents offering support and friendship to other bereaved parents and their families.

RELATE

Herbert Gray College

Little Church Street

Rugby

Warks CV21 3AP

www.relate.org.uk

Tel: 01788 573241 (office)

Fax: 01788 535007

Opening Times: (Mon-Fri, 9am-5pm)

Can put individuals in touch with local Relate centres, which offer counselling to couples experiencing relationship difficulties, including those who are not married. Payment according to circumstances.

BRITISH ASSOCIATION OF COUNSELLING AND PSYCHOTHERAPY (BACP)

BACP House

35-37 Albert Street

Rugby

Warks CV21 2SG

www.bacp.co.uk

E-mail: bacp@bacp.co.uk

Can provide a list of counsellors within a local area. Fees will vary according to counsellor.

NATIONAL FAMILY MEDIATION

9 Tavistock Place

London

WC1H 9SN

Tel: 020 7383 5993 (office)

Opening Times: (Mon-Fri, 9.30am-5pm)

For separating or divorcing couples. Can help couples make joint decisions about a range of issues, e.g. how to separate, what to say to the children, distribution of money and property. Provides details of local services.

NATIONAL ASSOCIATION OF CHILD
CONTACT CENTRES
Minerva House
Spaniel Row
Nottingham
NG1 6EP

www.naccc.org.uk
E-mail: contact@naccc.org.uk
Tel: 0115 948 4557 (office)
Fax: 0115 941 5519

Centres offer neutral meeting places where
children of separated families can enjoy
contact with one or both parents, and
sometimes other family members, in a
comfortable and safe environment when
there is no viable alternative.

GRANDPARENTS ASSOCIATION
01279 444964

GRANDPARENTS ACTION GROUP
01952 582621

Both groups help grandparents who want to
keep in touch with grandchildren affected by
separation and family change.

YOUNG MINDS
102-108 Clerkenwell Road
London
EC1M 5SA

Tel: 020 7336 8445 (office)
Tel: 0800 0182138 (helpline)
Opening Times: (Mon & Fri, 10am-1pm)
(Tues, Weds, Thurs, 1-4pm)

Free service for parents and carers who are
worried about the emotional well-being of
their child. Staff listen to issues of concern,
offer literature and tell people about local
services.

Index